I Remember
BOBBY JONES

I Remember
BOBBY JONES

*Personal Memories of and Testimonials to
Golf's Most Charismatic Grand Slam Champion,
as Told by the People Who Knew Him*

MIKE TOWLE

Cumberland House
Nashville, Tennessee

Published by Cumberland House Publishing, Inc., 431 Harding Industrial Drive,
Nashville, TN 37211 • www.cumberlandhouse.com

Cover design by Gore Studio, Inc.
Text design by Mary Sanford

Library of Congress Cataloging-in-Publication Data
Towle, Mike.
    I remember Bobby Jones : personal memories of and testimonials to golf's most
charismatic grand slam champion, as told by the people who knew him / [com-
piled by] Mike Towle.
       p. cm.
    Includes bibliographical references (p.) and index.

    1. Jones, Bobby, 1902–1971--Anecdotes. 2. Jones, Bobby, 1902–1971--
Friends and associates. 3. Golfers--United States--Biography. I. Title.

GV964.J6 T69 2001
796.352'092--dc21
[B]

                                                    2001017243

1 2 3 4 5 6 7—06 05 04 03 02 01
ISBN 978-1-58182-391-2 (pbk)

To Roy Carpenter and Grandpa Towle,
two fine golfers in their own right

Contents

ACKNOWLEDGMENTS

The following people were immensely helpful in making this book possible, especially considering the fact that many of the people who knew Bob Jones on a first-name basis are either deceased or too loyal to the what-you-see-and-hear-here-stays-here tenets of Augusta National Golf Club to be willing to speak about Jones on the record. My thanks go to Michael Arkush, Tommy Barnes, Frank Chirkinian, Frank Christian Jr., John Derr, Doug Ford, Bob Goalby, Freddie Haas, Lionel Hebert, Tommy Jacobs, Byron Nelson, Paul Runyan, Sam Snead, Louise Suggs, Charlie Yates, and Dan Yates.

My condolences go out to the Lionel Hebert family—Lionel, the 1957 PGA Championship winner, passed away on December 30, 2000. Just a few weeks earlier he had granted me what turned out to be a wonderful interview about his memories of Bob Jones, Augusta, and the Masters.

The folks at the Nashville Public Library were most gracious in helping me track down a variety of publications used as research for this project. I also thank those invisible, tiny people who work behind my computer screen in that netherworld known as the Internet: If you want a great search engine, try www.google.com. It's awesome.

As always, I thank my wife, Holley, and son, Andrew, for giving me the time and space to freely exercise my creative juices for this work. Much of what went into polishing up this work ate up a lot of what should have been family time during the Christmas holiday season. I also thank publisher Ron Pitkin, editor Mary Sanford, publicists Jennifer Martin and Stacie Bauerle, and the entire Cumberland House gang for their support. Thanks be to our Lord, Jesus Christ, too, for making all this possible and bearable.

INTRODUCTION

This book is for any golfer who, given a chance to pick three great golfers for his or her dream foursome, would leave Bobby Jones off the list. That would be a loss, borderline tragic. Take all the great golfers of the twentieth century, somehow devise an equal playing field of equipment and course conditions, and let's see what happens. Who would be the best? No matter how you slice it, Jones belongs in the top three, perhaps with Jack Nicklaus and Tiger Woods occupying the other two spots, with Sam Snead, Gene Sarazen, Ben Hogan, Arnold Palmer, and Byron Nelson battling it out for Mr. Congeniality.

Why Jones? Let me count the ways. One, Jones won his thirteen majors in an eight-year stretch before retiring at age twenty-eight; two, he could hit a ball more than three hundred yards with a hickory shaft; three, he loved playing with golfers of all abilities and giving helpful advice when asked; four, he had a good sense of humor; five, he wore knickers; and six, he was well versed in the extracurricular activities of golf often found at the nineteenth hole. Jones was the whole package, and he certainly had to be a fascinating conversationalist with three college degrees under his belt and a law practice, to boot.

Jones could flat-out play great golf. Plus there's a certain mystique about him, in part because of his cofounding role for Augusta National Golf Club and the Masters Tournament and the fact that he quit playing golf at age twenty-eight after spending eight consecutive years, unofficially and arguably, as the number one golfer in the world.

After giving up competitive golf at such an early age, Jones, unwittingly, didn't have a lot of years left for recreational golf either. He played his last full round of golf at his home course, East Lake Country Club, at the age of forty-five in 1947. One day after shooting an even-par 72 at East Lake, which included a double bogey on his seventeenth hole, Jones entered a hospital for exploratory surgery. The eventual prognosis was syringomyelia, a congenital disorder that disconnects the motor nerves in the body from the brain. Jones lived the last twenty-three years of his life gradually ravaged by this disease, although he rarely spoke about any part of his suffering with those around him.

This guy was human, even prone to tossing the occasional club. Yet his achievements were borderline superhuman.

Need a fourth, Mr. Jones?

I Remember
BOBBY JONES

THE ATLANTA CONNECTION

It has been more than seventy years since Bobby Jones completed his unprecedented, still unmatched feat of winning golf's four majors in the same calendar year. So much time has gone by, in fact, that it's easy to assume that Jones was only a great champion of long ago who spent the last forty years of his life holed up in Augusta, briefly showing up on TV once a year as a figurehead at the Masters Tournament. If we didn't know any better, it would be easy to draw the conclusion that Augusta was Jones's home—that he was born there, grew up there, and lived the rest of his life there. Nothing could be farther from the truth.

Jones was an Atlantan through and through. He grew up in Atlanta, calling East Lake Country Club in northwest Atlanta his home away from home. Jones learned the game at East Lake, developed his championship skills there, and went back there after he retired from golf to become "just another member" playing friendly rounds with others while practicing law in downtown Atlanta. If Augusta National was his dream club, East Lake was his home club, and it was there that he forged myriad friendships with other golfers of various ages and handicaps. It also was at East Lake that Jones, as a young boy, met a Scotsman from Carnoustie,

Jones at twenty-one, a Harvard student preparing for the 1923 U.S. Amateur. (AP/Wide World Photos)

Stewart Maiden, who would become young Jones's golfing mentor, teaching Jones the game more through osmosis and demonstration than outright instruction. The young Jones would often follow Maiden around the course, looking for swing keys and tendencies that he eagerly incorporated into his own game. Along the way, he put together a long, flowing, rhythmic swing that generated tremendous power with seemingly a minimal amount of effort.

Likewise, Jones was more than gracious in passing along the baton, in his retirement-from-golf years spending hours at East Lake showing the youthful likes of prominent-champions-to-be Louise Suggs, Charlie Yates, and Tommy Barnes the finer points of great golf. Jones wasn't only approachable with an open-door spirit, he would seek out the opportunity to play golf with young players who exhibited the passion and potential for good golf.

Jones was born on Saint Patrick's Day in 1902, the son of Atlanta attorney "Colonel" Bob Jones. The younger Jones was sickly as a child, and there was even some concern that he would not survive infancy. He was five years old when he was introduced to the game, and within ten years he had emerged as one of the top up-and-coming amateurs in the United States. At the age of fourteen, he qualified for the U.S. Amateur and made it all the way to the quarterfinals before losing. Another seven years would go by, however, before he would win his first major, the 1923 U.S. Open.

——————

Unlike other great golfers such as Byron Nelson and Ben Hogan who would follow him as mostly self-taught golfers, Jones had a golf mentor in the form of Stewart Maiden, whose free-flowing

swing became a Jones trademark, as explained by The Golf
Immortals *authors* **Tom Scott** *and* **Geoffrey Cousins.**
*Maiden, as far as can be determined, never gave Jones a formal
golf lesson, but he didn't need to. Playing lots of golf with little
Bobby tagging along was all that was needed, apparently:*

Jones's development was influenced by the fact that from
about the age of four or five he grew up in a golfing atmos-
phere, had a golfing father who suspected the existence of
talent and did his best to foster it. It would not be right to
say that Jones was self-taught. He learned mainly by example, and never had what might be called a set lesson or a set
of lessons. But during his formative years he had the advice,
the support, and the presence as model of a silent Scot from
Carnoustie, Stewart Maiden. Maiden had a leisurely, easy-
going swing without frills or sharp points, and the kid Bobby
gradually assimilated this particular method of playing the
game. There can be no doubt also that the youngster's obser-
vations, in his teens, of the style of Harry Vardon also helped
in developing his particular technique. But Maiden was the
original mold of his form.

Maiden's forte was teaching. He had the distinction of
influencing the early careers of two of America's greatest
golfers—Bobby Jones and Alexa Stirling, three times winner
of the United States women's championship. Maiden was a
man of few words but admirable fluency of swing. It wasn't
what he said, but what he did, which helped Bobby on the
road to fame.[1]

*In writing about Jones as a young man and sometimes enfant
terrible, renowned golf writer* **Herbert Warren Wind** *gives a
succinct biography of a young man who would overcome his bad
temper to become one of the true gentlemen of the game:*

In a country so overflowing with infant prodigies that the
child who couldn't break off a curve sharper than Matty's or
dash off a song hit or exhibit some other startling precocity
appeared to be an out-and-out case of arrested development,
Bobby Jones was the infant prodigy. He had taken up golf at
five. His mother and his dad, a well-to-do Atlanta lawyer,
had joined the East Lake Golf Club that summer, and while
they learned their fundamentals from Jimmy Maiden, Bobby
knocked a ball up and down a road bordering the course. A
digestive ailment had prevented him from eating any substantial food until he was five, and Bobby was a frail, thin little fellow. The next summer the Joneses took a cottage on
the East Lake property near the old thirteenth green. Bobby
used to follow his parents around the course, batting the ball
with a cut-down cleek, worried more about keeping up with
the grownups' pace than hitting the ball correctly. He liked
to follow the new pro, Jimmy Maiden's brother Stewart, but
Stewart paid no attention to the little fellow with the over-
sized head and, after being ignored for five or six holes,
Bobby would wander home.[2]

*Growing up in the early 1900s, Bobby Jones was decades away
from having the advantage of video golf instructionals, let alone
live television coverage of golf events and even instructional
books, which were in comparatively short supply in his day. Like*

7

*other golfers of his golf-pioneering generation, much of what
Jones learned about golf came from watching and emulating
skilled, older golfers he was exposed to as a boy and young man
growing up in Atlanta. Even then, Jones cautioned against being
too reliant on an expert instructor when it came to learning or
fine-tuning one's golf game:*

It is not easy to teach golf either by personal instruction or
by writing. In order to play well, the player must have the
feel of the proper stroke. Being unable to view himself objec-
tively, he has no other guide than the sensations produced by
the action of his muscles. Yet the words in our language that
we must use to describe feel are necessarily vague and sus-
ceptible to varying interpretations among different persons;
so that no one can describe the feel of a muscular action with
assurance that the description will be readily and inevitably
understood by another. For this reason, I think it is necessary
in all forms of golf instruction to repeat over and over
descriptions of the same movements, all the while altering
the modes of expression and terms of reference. Often the
learner will grasp the teacher's meaning when stated in one
way when he has failed to understand it in many other
forms.[3]

*Although Jones did not find golf to be a great source of fascina-
tion for him in the early going, it didn't take him long to discover
the joy of victory, and it was a favorite sentiment that would
stay with him for many years:*

The first competitive golf I played was at the age of six years, when I won my first cup. . . . I have it today (1927), and I'll keep it always; a tiny cup three inches tall, and a cup that I'll always feel I'm not entitled to keep.

There was a party at Mrs. Meador's when our family was living there. Alexa Stirling, who later won the women's national championship three times in succession, lived in the neighborhood, and Frank Meador of course lived at the same house I did, and Perry Adair was invited and Mrs. Meador arranged a medal competition; six holes on the old East Lake course, and provided this little cup as the trophy . . . If Mr. Maeterlinck is right, and if the past, present, and future really are co-existent, I'd love to go over that round of six holes again and check it up. Because I'll always believe Alexa won that cup. Frank Meador, however, figured it out that I won it, and as his mother was giving the cup, we regarded Frank as having something like a plenary connection to it, so it was awarded to me . . . I took it to bed with me that night . . . I've a hundred and twenty cups and vases now, and thirty medals, but there's one little cup that never fails of being kept well polished. And I never slept with another one.[4]

Renowned sportswriter **Grantland Rice** *was one of the early members of Augusta National and a Jones crony who wrote* The Bobby Jones Story, *published in 1953 as an adaptation from the writings of* **O. B. Keeler.** *As Rice and Keeler point out, one of the watershed moments in young Jones's burgeoning career was the time he finally shot as low as 80 at East Lake's old course, a tough venue that included only two par-threes, both of which were among the first three holes played, making* *the last fifteen a rough go for a young lad of ten struggling as it was just to break 90 each time out:*

On this summer day, he (Jones) was playing with Perry (Adair, another highly regarded youth, three years senior to Jones) as usual, but for once—and for the first time—he wasn't paying any attention to what Perry was doing. He was scoring better than he ever had scored before and he had no room in his mind for anything else. At the last green, faced with a four-foot putt for an even 80, he must have wondered why his skinny little chest was so tight and why his hands were trembling as he stood up to that putt, not to beat Perry but just to score an 80. Down went the putt and on the card went the 80, with the signature of Perry Adair on the attested line.

And away across the golf course went Bobby Jones, setting off at a brisk trot to find his dad. He found Big Bob at the fourteenth green, and he walked solemnly up to him and held out the card—without a word—his hand still trembling. Big Bob took the card and looked at it. Then he looked at Bobby. Then he put his arms around him and hugged him hard. And so before he was a dozen years old, Bobby Jones had discovered a new adversary in golf, the Great Opponent whose tangible form is only a card and a pencil. He had played his first round against the toughest foeman of them all—Old Man Par.[5]

As good a story line as Jones's golfing career makes, he was not an instant sensation after being introduced to the game. As he himself points out, it was a sport that didn't make a big

Atlanta Mayor I. W. Ragsdale greets Jones upon the latter's return home after winning the 1929 U.S. Open at Winged Foot. (AP/Wide World Photos)

impression on him—at first—and he could just as easily have forged a future in another sport:

I wish I could say here that a strange thrill shot through my skinny little bosom when I swung at a golf ball for the first

11

time; but it wouldn't be truthful. I do not remember the first time I hit a golf ball, or hit at one; and as I recall it the game did not make much of an impression on me, except that I used to get mad enough to dance in the road when a wild shot went under a little bridge covered with briers across the ditch, which was not the second hole. I liked baseball much better, and played golf, or what we called golf, because of a dearth of boys in the neighborhood with whom to play baseball.[6]

In getting to know Jones, **Clifford Roberts** *also got to know Jones's family as well, including Bobby's father:*

Bob was very devoted to the Colonel (Jones's dad, Robert Purmetus Jones) and treated him with the utmost respect. The Colonel was extremely proud of his son and was always ready to make any financial sacrifice that might be necessary in order that Bob could travel to golf tournaments as much as he liked. The same thing applied to Bob's wishes about schooling. I doubt if Bob could ever have done anything that pleased the Colonel quite as much as when he once declined a fine home in Atlanta that had been offered to him, as a present, by some well-meaning and generous-minded friends.

Enjoying their very close father-and-son relationship, both the Colonel and Bob were anxious to spend as much time together as possible. But their inclinations and attitudes were decidedly dissimilar in some respects. The Colonel might properly be described as an extrovert in that he was outgoing and friendly with everyone, including strangers, and was invariably the leader at group gatherings in fun making, storytelling, and singing. Bob, on the other hand, was definitely a conservative, and on a number of occasions, when the Colonel was unusually rambunctious, was made to feel uncomfortable or even embarrassed.[7]

---

*Although Augusta National is notorious for its tight-lipped privacy and exclusively male makeup of its membership, Jones was a visible proponent for all golfers, male and female, young and adult. Along with everything else, Jones was an approachable person who often sought out people to join him for a round of golf, his accessibility no more evident than when he was back home in Atlanta on the friendly confines of his native East Lake Country Club. There, one of the many young golfers with whom Jones made his acquaintance was **Louise Suggs,** twenty-one years his junior. Suggs, however, was no ordinary golfer in her own right. Even before becoming one of the founding members of the LPGA in 1950, she had carved out a spectacular career that included victories in the 1947 U.S. Women's Amateur, the 1946 and 1947 Western Amateur Championship and Western Open, the 1946 Titleholders, and the 1948 British Amateur. Like Jones a native of Atlanta, Suggs grew up among a number of area amateurs who made the mark regionally as well as nationally as some of the top amateurs in the United States. All of them had ties to Jones, who was as genuinely gracious to youngsters as he was to adults when it came to sharing his knowledge of the game. Suggs looks back on her golfing association with Jones, which included many rounds played together:*

His father and my grandfather had some business dealings together when I was a young girl. That's how I met him.

13

After he won the Grand Slam, they had a parade for him in Atlanta, and I remember being there. We were on the porch of the Capital City Club on Peachtree Street, and that's really my first recollection of Bobby Jones. At that point, golf didn't really mean anything to me.

My father was a professional ballplayer and my grandparents owned a professional baseball club in Atlanta. Then Dad got into golf and built a nine-hole golf course on the outskirts of Atlanta. He called it Lithia Springs. This was in 1932, in the middle of the depression. Naturally, Bobby Jones's name in Atlanta was like the King of England's, you might say. I don't remember specifically how I met him as far as golf is concerned. What I do remember is playing golf at East Lake Country Club, and on Sundays they would have mixed-team matches or whatever they called them, and I played with him in that a number of times. I was in my teens then. That's because his wife, Mary, didn't play golf. I won the state amateur title when I was sixteen and won the Southern when I was seventeen, so I wasn't too bad a golfer, I guess. I played with him on other occasions as well. I'd go out there after work and he'd be there and would say, "C'mon, let's go and play a few holes." When I turned pro in July of 1948, and I can't tell you how it happened, but the first exhibition I played as a professional was with him and two other men at Highlands Country Club in Highlands, North Carolina.

I remember one time, when I was about eighteen or nineteen years old, asking him, "If you had one piece of advice for me, what would it be?" And he said, "Just knock hell out of it; it'll come down somewhere." I guess he said that to his son, too; he was a big strong boy and could knock the ball a mile. We talked a lot about golf, but not so much the technical side of it. I remember playing alone with him one time just messing around with our games. At one point I ended up behind a tree about 150 yards from the green and after looking at it for a while, I said, "Mr. Jones, how would you play this shot?" And he said, "Well, how do you want to play it?" He proceeded to hook a ball around the tree, slice a ball around it, hit one over it, and hit one under its branches. Not only did he demonstrate each shot, he made it look like there was hardly any effort involved in doing it. He then said, "You've got four options. What do you want to do?" That was the kind of guy he was.

Most people now don't realize what golf really is. They think it's just hit it hard, chase it again, and get it into the hole. In those days, we didn't have the manicured golf courses they have now. If we got a decent lie, we were very fortunate. I see fairways nowadays that are better than some of the greens we putted on. We were shotmakers in those days. We had to be. In order to do that, you had to be able to use your hands in more ways than one. Most of the guys and gals now just knock the hell out of it and wait for it to come down. In light of all this, one of the things I think about when talking about Tiger Woods is that he has so much of an imagination that it's not even funny. This is what that young man has seen his whole life, and when he's faced with a shot that won't work from a normal standpoint, he creates something. That's what we used to do, and Tiger does it so well.

<hr>

*Another of the young golfers who practically grew up at Jones's knee at East Lake was **Tommy Barnes,** who would go on to* win a couple of Southern Amateurs among his many victories in a sterling amateur career. He also qualified for the U.S. Amateur sixteen times, although he never won it. One of Barnes's many other impressive feats in golf was shooting a course-record 62 at East Lake—at the age of seventy-three, breaking the old record of 63 set by Jones decades earlier. Barnes also has the distinction of having played with Jones during Jones's last eighteen-hole round of golf at East Lake in 1948, with Jones all the while holding on to a secret that would be revealed in the next day's newspapers. Barnes takes us back to his early days at East Lake and on through to the final round he played with Jones:

I won the state amateur when I was fifteen years old, and about a month later I got a letter from the East Lake club president offering me a membership out there. This was in 1931 and twenty-five years later, in 1956, I found out that Bob Jones had gone to one of the club's directors to ask them to give me that club membership. I got a chance during the thirties to play some golf with Bob at East Lake, and he was about the greatest person I ever met in my life. He was the most humble guy you could have met: If you didn't know what he had won during his competitive career, you certainly wouldn't find out from him.

One thing I learned from Bob was that he didn't really start learning how to win until 1923, which was when he learned that in order to win he couldn't worry about the game of the other competitors and that he had to be concerned only with his game. And that was the year that he won the first of his thirteen majors (starting with the 1923 U.S. Open, where he beat Bobby Cruickshank in a playoff). As he wrote it up in his book, he ended up playing Old Man

Par, and Old Man Par never made a birdie, and he never made a bogey either. In fact, it had been reported that before then he had been really friendly with all of his fellow competitors. I remember hearing that, sometime later at Augusta, some guys were in the locker room talking about that very thing when Gene Sarazen walked in and said, "I'll guarantee you that he was about the nicest person there is to play golf with, even if he was your opponent."

All I know is that Bob was very friendly toward me and helped me with my game because he was the kind of person who would play with anybody, regardless of their handicap. In fact, we gambled pretty heavily at times during the 1930s playing one-dollar Nassaus with a four-dollar limit. You could bet anything that teeing off at number one Bob was playing just as hard as he would have been if he had been playing in the National Open. After the war (World War II), where he served on General Eisenhower's staff as an intelligence officer in England because he wanted to serve his country, he was still playing super golf as a plus-four handicap. We would usually try to get up a game every Sunday morning in which Charlie Yates (likewise a nationally ranked amateur out of Atlanta) played against Bob and his partner. Somebody once asked me, "How was it playing with him?" and I said, "Well, there was good news and there was bad news. The good news was that I got to play golf with one of the greatest golfers and fellows who had ever lived, and the bad news was that I never got him for a partner."

They had a place in the locker room cut out for him where he could have some privacy, but if you went down there and walked past him, he would invite you over to sit down and have a drink with him. I was too young, so I would only have a coke with him. Now he might have had some corn liquor down there somewhere, but I didn't indulge in it. O. B. Keeler (Jones's good friend and chronicler) had a wooden leg, and folks said that when they played there, that's where they kept the whiskey—in his wooden leg.

You couldn't help but improve your own game while playing with him a lot. If you didn't improve your game playing with him, you'd get clobbered. One of the best things that ever happened to me was getting that club membership because that allowed me to play a lot with guys like Bob and Charlie Yates. They had all the top players from around there playing out there. One thing about Bob was that he would never say something like, "This is the way to play." It was more like, "Well, this is the way that I play." He was a prince of a fellow.

I played the last round with Bob in 1948 at East Lake. I was in a foursome with Bob; the assistant pro at the club Henry Linder; and one of the club's board directors, Bob Ingram. It was the two Bobs against Henry and me. I will never forget it. Bob was two under par with two holes to go, and then he hit the only bad drive I ever saw him hit in my life. He duck-hooked it over into the woods at number eight and took a double, before he parred nine—we had played the back nine first—so he ended up with an even-par 72. Then the next day I read in the newspaper that he was going into the Emory University Hospital for some exploratory tests because he had been experiencing some numbness in his limbs. I found out several years ago from Randy Waters, the sports editor at Channel 5 here in Atlanta, who called me up one time and asked me if I knew of anyone else living who had known Jones, and I told him about Henry Leonard. Anyway, he got in touch with Henry, who by now was down in Florida, and he came up to East Lake and we sat out there behind number eighteen while he asked us questions about what had gone on back in those days. That's when Henry said something that I had never heard talked about. Henry said that at number one, after we had played the back nine first, that the three of us hit our drives all the way down to the bottom of the hill there. And while we were waiting for the group ahead of us to get off the green before we hit our second shots, Henry went over to Bob and noticed that Bob had a four-iron in his hands. Henry said, "Mr. Jones, I've been watching you all the way around and you and I have been hitting the same club every time, but now I notice you've got a four and I'm going to hit a five." That's when Bob said, "Henry, I've been noticing some numbness in my limbs." I had never heard that before that recent interview because Henry had moved away and we never discussed it. The next day is when I noticed the story in the sports section of the newspaper about Bob having some tests that day.

I went over to the hospital later that same week and after walking down the hall, I saw a sign over his room that said No Admittance. So I turned around and started walking back up the hall when I ran into his father coming down the hall and I said, "How is he doing, Colonel?" and he said, "He's heavily sedated." And I said, "Well, I'll come back later," and he said, "No, go on in because I know he'd love to see you." So I went in and saw the big patch on the back of his neck where they had already been doing some exploratory tests, I guess. After that, he just went down and down and down. It's amazing how he was able to play that last round—the man was crippled and he still shot a 72.

Spalding had a retail store downtown on Broad Street, and his law office close by. I was going to the Spalding store that next day when I saw him coming down the street. We stopped each other and talked for a few minutes and I said, "Bob, I was sorry to hear about your problem." And he said, "Well, I've been having the problem for several months." I had never heard of anybody having that disease (syringomyelia) but him.

Dan Yates, whose older brother Charlie Yates was one of America's top amateur golfers for many years, also recalls the days of yesteryear spent at East Lake Country Club getting to know Jones and being groomed for the game of a lifetime. Both Dan and Charlie Yates eventually became members of Augusta National and became pressroom fixtures during Masters week, emceeing press conferences featuring Masters contenders. Both men, now in their eighties, still live in Atlanta, never far removed from their roots at East Lake and their memories of Bob Jones:

Charles was just a teenager when he started playing with Jones. He was a pretty good player back in those early days. We lived right across the street from the fourth tee at East Lake, and we would be hanging around out there beating golf balls from the time that we were five or six years old. When other kids were out playing football and baseball, we were out there playing golf. When Charles would play with Bob Jones, I would just kind of tag behind. I must have been about eight or ten at the time. He played every Saturday in a foursome with Bob that also included Bob's dad, Colonel Bob, and the local preacher from the First Methodist Church, and they would have some great matches with Charles and the preacher teamed against Bob and the

Colonel. But even as great a player as Jones had been and considering how idolized a man he was, he never acted like someone who knew he was being idolized. He was just a very friendly, approachable person with no airs about him. He was just an ordinary fellow who liked to play golf with the members. In the locker room they had established a sort of enlarged area for Bob, but he would just sit there and chat with anybody who came by.

He was just like one of your good friends. He treated us kids so good, often giving us a golf ball or some golf clubs— that sort of thing. I never knew a finer gentleman than Bob Jones. To think that he won all of those tournaments playing hickory-shafted clubs, with which he could hit the ball over three hundred yards when he wanted to. Who knows what he could have done with the equipment they now use. One of the clubs I remember buying around 1934, when I was about sixteen, was a steel-shafted sand wedge that Spalding had made, and it was one that Bob had designed. There were a number of other clubs that he gave me over the years. I'm just sorry I didn't keep some of the ones he gave me. After he went with Spalding in the early 1930s, he used to get all these clubs from Spalding and he had them in this big golf bag he kept in his huge locker. We had the option of going in there and getting a club to try out and if we liked it, he would give it to us. We called it his Grab Bag. His wood clubs were so heavy, though, that I couldn't play with them.

There were a lot of really good golfers that came out of East Lake, guys with scratch or plus handicaps. Years earlier there had been a streetcar line that stopped right in front of the club, and the members would bring their wives or girlfriends out to East Lake for the weekend. One of the main attractions in those days was a paddlewheel boat that operated out on the lake. They'd also come out to fish and picnic. Then in 1904 they built a golf course there. Then they brought in Donald Ross to redo the course, which, I guess, was in the late teens or early twenties. Later on, Tom Cousins's foundation bought the course and the clubhouse. There was a local housing project where the number two course was located. He was able to tear down the old slum areas there and he built new housing. And he built another golf course over there, which is about a par 62 or 63, and he named it the Charlie Yates Golf Club. The East Lake golf course is in much better condition now than it had been for a long time. After he took it over, he got Rees Jones to redo the course. He couldn't find the original drawings, but he got some of the golfers who remembered the original course to go out there—like Tommy Barnes and my brother Charlie—to gather out there and offer suggestions based on their memories. This was six or seven years ago. They didn't put the course back to exactly as it had originally been designed by Donald Ross, but it was pretty close. They've now had the PGA Tour Championship there twice, and the course is back in magnificent condition.

I don't think there has ever been a better golfer than Bob Jones, irrespective of Tiger Woods or anybody else. I just think you can't really compare different eras. But Bob was more dominant in his day than Tiger has been. He would give us kids tips on the game. There were two things he told me in particular that I remember to this day. One is, when you stand over a golf ball getting ready to hit it, you can't think about more than one thing at a time. The other thing I've always tried to remember is to stay behind the ball with your hands. He'd give us tips and watch us hit balls. He's been an idol all of my life, to tell you the truth. And, fortunately, he let me join Augusta in 1960. My brother Charles has been a member longer than anybody, having joined in 1940.

After the war, in 1946, Bob got together with some of his friends and built Peachtree Golf Club, which is in northwest Atlanta. He got Robert Trent Jones to design the course, although Bob was out there much of the time to see what was going on and to offer his ideas to some of the things that were going on, in much the same way he had done with Alister Mackenzie at Augusta. It was made into a fine facility. In fact, they had the Walker Cup Matches there in 1989, when my son, Danny, happened to be a member of the U.S. team that year. Bob had been there during the building of the golf course to hit some shots to check things out, but by the time they finished it he couldn't play anymore. Jones had also been crazy about St. Andrews. He once said that if he had had only the experience of playing St. Andrews, he would have had a full golfing life.

---

*As for the Yates brothers, now it's **Charlie Yates**'s turn to look back on his long friendship with Jones. Yates went on to win the 1938 British Amateur and ended up as low amateur at the Masters Tournament four times:*

We moved out to East Lake when I was a youngster, and one of the first things about Bob Jones that sticks out in my mind was when he lost the 1925 U.S. Open by one stroke. I saw him back at the East Lake clubhouse about a week after he had lost that match (to Willie Macfarlane, 147-148, in a thirty-six-hole playoff). I said to him, "I'm sorry that you

I REMEMBER BOBBY JONES

lost," and he said, "Don't worry. Forget about it, son, because the good thing is you don't know who your friends are until you lose." That really made an impression on me.

———⟨⟨⟨⟩⟩⟩———

As most people know, Jones earned three college degrees including a law degree, and he practiced law for a number of years in Atlanta following his retirement from competitive golf. Long-time Jones friend and frequent playing partner **Tommy Barnes** *gives this brief, secondhand description of Jones's law practice:*

They tell the story of the time he was trying a case at a little town down in south Georgia somewhere. The judge was a golfer and while Jones was down there, the judge asked Bob to go to lunch with him. So Bob did, then came back and won the case. After he got back to Atlanta, Bob told some people that he couldn't be trying cases like this anymore because he felt he was taking advantage of people. I didn't know if it's true or not, but I heard he never tried another case after that. That's the kind of person he was. He was so well known and such a likable person to boot, that he must have felt that maybe he was getting a little leeway, and that that wasn't right.

———⟨⟨⟨⟩⟩⟩———

2

GRAND SLAM CHAMPION

Seven years elapsed between the time Jones first attained national prominence as a fourteen-year-old advancing to the quarterfinals of the U.S. Amateur and his first major victory, that being his victory at the 1923 U.S. Open. Jones defeated Bobby Cruickshank in a playoff to win the '23 Open at Inwood Country Club on Long Island, New York. In becoming only the fourth amateur to win the Open, Jones acted more relieved than ecstatic, saying, "I don't care what happens to me now, ever." The relief was from ending his seven-year "drought" in light of a popular catch phrase that had said Jones was "the greatest golfer in the world, but he can't win."

Jones made up for lost time, and it was quickly apparent that he *did* care what happened to him. Beginning with that 1923 Open victory, Jones won a total of thirteen major championships over eight years, culminating in his 1930 "Impregnable Quadrilateral," whereby he won the U.S. and

British Opens and the U.S. and British Amateurs. In other words, it was a "Grand Slam," the only one-year slam recorded in men's major-championship golf during the twentieth century. Modern-day cynics question the validity of Jones's Grand Slam, pointing out that two of the majors of that time were amateur events. True, they were, but even as late as 1930 golf's amateur ranks were, at worst, equal in caliber to the pro ranks. Winning a national amateur championship was every bit as difficult as winning an Open.

Very few golfers other than Walter Hagen could make a respectable living as a touring professional, and most serious golfers had to forge careers in other fields while keeping amateur golf championship as a second priority. Jones never did compete as a pro, retiring at the age of twenty-eight after completing his slam in 1930. With three degrees in hand, including a law degree from Harvard, Jones transitioned from competitive golf to a career as an Atlanta attorney. But he was better known as the cofounder of the Augusta National Golf Club and a prestigious invitational tournament that came to be known as the Masters.

Only two of Jones's four Grand Slam victories of 1930 retain that major status—the U.S. and British Opens. The national amateur championships have effectively been replaced on the list of Grand Slam events by the Masters and the PGA Championship, meaning no amateur will ever pull off a contemporary version of Jones's one-year slam because amateurs don't compete in the PGA. Still, through 2000, no golfer, amateur or professional, had won all four modern-day majors in the same year. Only two, Ben Hogan and Tiger Woods, had won three of the four in the same year. Only five—Hogan, Woods, Jack Nicklaus, Gary Player, and Gene Sarazen—have each won all four Slam events in their careers. Only Nicklaus has topped Jones's career mark of thirteen major triumphs, having totaled eighteen—twenty, if you count Nicklaus's two U.S. Amateur victories. Therefore, an argument can be made that Jones was the best of the Grand Slam champs.

Jones's championship legacy isn't measured only in Grand Slam victories; it also is measured in the man, a gracious winner who learned how to harness a terrible temper that had plagued him in his teenage years. Some had even called him a spoiled brat. But Jones not only learned how to squelch his demons, he re-emerged in his twenties as, at least in public, the epitome of sportsmanship in victory as well as defeat, although there weren't many of the latter. Jones's impact on the game was such that later in life he became only the second American ever made an Honorary Burgess of the Borough by the people of St. Andrews in Scotland. The first? Benjamin Franklin. Added Jones, who years earlier had been greeted by two thousand residents in 1936 when he showed up for a round of golf at St. Andrews with some old friends, "If I take out of my life everything except my experiences at St. Andrews, I'd still have had a rich, full life."

⸻

Herbert Warren Wind saw beneath Jones's calming veneer a gritty competitor who unwittingly took pounds off his frame at the same time he was shaving strokes off his scores:

While Bobby had never won a major title (as of 1922, going into the U.S. Open), the consistent excellence of his golf stamped him as the nation's leading amateur. The press and the public agreed that he was fulfilling the promise of his earlier

27

youth and was bound to break through to a glorious triumph sooner or later. Bobby could not share those sanguine feelings. His shots had never really caught fire during a championship, yet year in and year out he had played good enough golf to win, but he hadn't. He resigned himself to the probability that something would always pop up to prevent him from winning—that is, if he continued to play in tournaments. On more than one occasion, Bobby was on the verge of retiring from competitive golf, a game so grueling for him that he lost as many as eighteen pounds during a championship with no victory to compensate for the punishment.[1]

Writer **Charles Price** *puts things in perspective in looking back to the Roaring Twenties, which also were known as "the Golden Age of Sports" for good reason:*

Even among sportswriters Jones had been a singular hero in a decade when they had a lot to choose from: Ruth, Grange, Dempsey, Tilden, Sande, Weismuller, Paddock, and, yes, Hagen. He had flashing good looks, a personality that could charm the blossoms off a peach tree, and the thoughtful grace of a man twice his age. (Who else might have been retired at twenty-eight, having set a record so improbable that nobody then could bring it into proper perspective?) But what really set Jones apart from all the other athletes of his day, and from all the other golfers before or since him, was not so much his educated intelligence, although that had a lot to do with it, nor his modesty, although that had something to do with it, nor his native talent, although without that we might not be privileged to be reading this book. No, what really set him apart was his insight into the game, gorgeous in its dimensions if you have waded through the treacle and sophisms of many of the golf books which have preceded this one, the authors of which, unlike Jones, had as much to do with the actual writing of them as King James did with writing the Holy Bible.[2]

Grantland Rice was not only the preeminent sportswriter of his day, he also was one of the early members of Augusta National Golf Club and a close friend of Jones's, back in the day when fraternization between journalists and the sports figures they covered was not considered taboo. Rice had a terrific vantage point from which to view Jones on and off the golf course, and he had no hesitation in singing the praises of Augusta's resident champion cofounder:

Almost one person in every ten million might have an interesting autobiography to put out at the age of twenty-five. Bobby Jones in this respect is one among ten million. This is supposed to be the age of youth in sport, but Bobby was the super-youth; for he was almost a seasoned competitor meeting and beating champions, at the age of fourteen. The entire history of sport has never recorded another such incident. At the age of twenty-five Bobby Jones had had thirteen years of campaigning. At the same age he had won almost every championship known to golf, through a vivid personal experience few competitors ever get to know at the age of sixty.[3]

Jones was not an overnight sensation as a golfer, and part of his problem in his early years of development—other than a temper he eventually reined in—was not realizing that his greatest opponent in golf was not the other guy or gal:

I never won a major championship until I learned to play golf against something, and not somebody. And that something was par . . . It took me many years to learn that, and a good deal of heartache.[4]

Another ingredient that went into making Jones such a charismatic champion was a healthy dose of humility, which is not a word he uses here in describing himself although he gets the point across:

Please don't understand me as being unappreciative of my good fortune in the matter of championship. But that is part of what I mean. There was so much of fortune, so much of luck, in my winning that I now feel more than ever that the popular value of championship is a factitious rating; and that golf is too great and too fine a game, and too much an epitome of life itself, for such a ranking to do it justice . . . I can speak frankly about this, now that I have won some spurs. I can say with all my heart that it means a great deal to me, for my name to be on three of the four [soon to be four of four] major golfing trophies of the world. And I can also say with all my heart that I think it's a rotten shame for us so readily to overlook the fine fellows and the truly great golfers who for one reason or another never have got within that charmed circle of national championship.[5]

Biographer **Dick Miller** *learned this about Jones in researching the great golfer:*

At the start of a match, Jones would approach his opponent, look at him straight in the eyes, shake his hand, and offer a quizzical smile that implied good luck. If the opponent looked at the smile long enough, however, its meaning became clearer. It said: *Good luck. You're going to need it because I'm going to beat the hell out of you today.*[6]

In being so closely affiliated with Jones for so many years, **Clifford Roberts** *gained some insights about the man that few others would have had the opportunity to ascertain:*

Bob never went into severe training in order to be at his best at any particular time. He felt that gymnastics were all very well in connection with many sports, but that golf required a different kind of muscular strength. He did no calisthenics and did not even care to walk as a method of exercise. Possibly one reason for this was varicose vein troubles, which required surgery several times. He was a moderately heavy cigarette smoker who always liked one before breakfast. He took a drink, preferably bourbon, whenever he felt like it, and, while I've seen him on special occasions indulge fairly liberally, he never lost control of his faculties.

Bob Jones was invariably considerate of his companions on the golf course, in the locker room, and elsewhere. He was a lot more interested in playing with people he liked than with the experts. His dad was invited to be a member of Bob's foursome more than anyone else. Bob was a good listener at the dinner table. Rarely did he interfere with the trend of the conversation, except if someone should tell a story that was just altogether too coarse and without any real humor. Whenever he undertook to contribute something, it was worthy of attention in that he was both a splendid raconteur and always able to provide fresh viewpoints on current topics. He had a wonderful sense of humor, and was simply incapable of being other than a gentleman at all times. In short, his character was the epitome of honor and integrity.[7]

Jones, perhaps more than any other golf-swing expert in history, had a flair with words and phrases when discussing the swing and swing keys, as he does here:

I like to think of a golf club as a weight attached to my hands by an imponderable medium, to which a string is a close approximation, and I like to feel that I am throwing it at the ball with much the same motion I should use in cracking a whip. By the simile, I mean to convey the idea of a supple and lightning-quick action of the wrists in striking—a sort of flailing action.[8]

How many times have amateur golfers been told by better, more-experienced golfers that the best way to strike a golf ball is by hitting down on the ball rather than through it? Jones gives his own analysis of the subject:

Expert players have discovered that the maximum length

from the tee, or when playing a ball lying well in the fairway, can be obtained by causing the club to strike the ball at or slightly in front of the lowest point in the arc of the swing. The notion that a golf ball can be made to fly carrying over-spin is pure fantasy, but when the ball is struck squarely in the back with the club moving parallel to the ground, or slightly upward, a minimum of backspin results. A ball so struck will fly in an arching trajectory so that it will still have some run left in it when it returns to the ground. A ball struck in this way will also have a greater capability of bor-ing into a headwind . . .

The player who tries, with any wood club, to get a ball up from a cuppy lie by getting the club under it in order to hit it upward is doomed to disappointment. He must either strike the ground first, or missing that, with the club coming up, hit the ball on top. This kind of shot can be played only by smashing the ball down so that the spin will cause it to rise. This is why, as you may have noticed, it is easier to play from a tight lie on level ground than on an upward slope. The need for the descending arc remains the same, but the slope, which at first blush would seem a help, makes the han-dling of the body movement more difficult.[9]

Charles Price, *in his foreword to the book* Bobby Jones on Golf, *discusses the fact that Jones retired at the ripe young age of twenty-eight after dominating world golf for the previous eight years, winning thirteen major championships in that span, includ-ing the 1930 "Impregnable Quadrilateral" that consisted of the U.S. and British Opens and the U.S. and British Amateurs:*

It would be the most natural assumption in the world to think that during those eight years Bobby Jones did little other than play golf. In reality, Jones played less formal golf during his championship years than virtually all of the players he beat, and he beat everybody in the world worth beating. Excepting the three seasons when he journeyed to Scotland or England for Walker Cup matches and, while there, the British championships, he spent most of the tournament season playing inconsequential matches with his father and an assortment of cronies at East Lake, his home club in Atlanta, where his interests and activities ranged far beyond matters of golf. Often, he would go for months without so much as picking up a club. Instead, he studied

Bobby and his dad, "Colonel" Bob Jones, enjoy another victory, this time young Bob's triumph in the 1927 British Open at St. Andrews. (AP/Wide World Photos)

mechanical engineering at Georgia Tech, got a degree in English literature at Harvard, dabbled in real estate, and then attended law school at Emory University. Midway through his second year, he took the state bar examinations, passed them, and so quit school to practice. As a result of these off-course activities, Jones averaged no more than three months a year playing in, and going to and from, tournaments and championships.[10]

Legendary golf teacher and best-selling author **Harvey Penick** *says that of all the great shots in golf he was privy to, there were none greater than the one he saw Jones strike at a second-echelon tournament back sometime in the 1920s:*

Bobby Jones hit the best shot I ever saw in a tournament. I was playing in the group 150 yards behind him at East Lake in Atlanta at the Southern Open and had a clear view.

On the seventh hole there is a big canyon on the right of the green with a grassy hollow at the bottom. The weather had been nasty, and suddenly hailstones as big as marbles began falling. The whole green was covered with hailstones. Jones had been down in the grassy hollow, but had pitched the ball just to the crown of the hill where he could hardly tell a golf ball from a hailstone. From there, he chipped the ball among the hailstones and it rolled right into the cup— for a par.

Jones had a way of doing whatever was necessary. Jack Burke Sr. said that to win a tournament the Lord has to put His hand on your head. This happened to Jones over and over.[11]

Ben Crenshaw, his knowledge of golf history unsurpassed by any other professional golfer of his generation, is well aware that there was more to Jones and his great record than what meets the eye:

One of the reasons for Jones's early retirement was the fact that he was inwardly high strung. So much that he regularly would lose ten to fifteen pounds during a championship. So much that his only form of relaxation would be to ingest two stiff drinks and soak in a hot tub of water. When a championship was over, he would burst into tears without provocation. Jones had a hell of a temper during his early years, regularly tossing clubs about, and once tore up his scorecard during his first British Open in 1921 at the course he would come to admire the most—the Old Course at St. Andrews. Somehow he learned to control his temper, and began winning the championships everyone expected him to win for such a long time, starting with the 1923 U.S. Open at Inwood on Long Island.[12]

Testimonies written to Jones's greatness flourished following his retirement from competitive golf in 1930 at the tender age of twenty-eight, as was the case in this excerpt of a piece Francis Powers wrote in the December 1930 issue of Golfer's Magazine:

Bob Jones was as much a genius with the bulger-faced woods and the curved irons as ever was Caruso to grand opera or Pavlova to the ballet. His like may never again be seen in the world of sport for no man ever dominated his field quite as much as the soft-spoken Georgian. Those of us who saw him in his meteoric championship years have been fortunate. We will have much to recall in the years to come.

Jones's retirement came unexpectedly. It was thought he would occasionally return to the green fields of contest for a tilt with par. But he has closed the door against such a probability and when Jones makes a decision it usually is a final one.[13]

———

Jones believed the complicated details of a golf swing were nothing more than the exercise of a basic scientific principle:

There is nothing occult about hitting a golf ball. In fact, although the application may be a bit more complicated, we use no more than the ordinary principles of motion we encounter numberless times every day. Once started upon a correct path, the club will tend to hold to its course until outside forces cause a change.[14]

———

Jones also offered some nifty advice about putting:

When you see a man obviously trying to guide the short putt, or hitting quickly with a short, stabbing stroke, even though he may hole a few, it will not be long before he meets trouble. A short putt, even as a long one, must be struck with a smooth, unhurried, and confident stroke. The best way to accomplish this is to decide upon a line to the hole and to determine to hit the ball on that line and let it go hang if it wants to. I have never had any better advice in golf, from tee to green, than was contained in a telegram sent me by

Stewart Maiden (Jones's childhood golf instructor) in 1919. It read: " Hit 'em hard. They'll land somewhere." You must not apply this advice literally to putting, but its application is obvious. Hit the putt as well as you can, and do not allow worry over the outcome to spoil the stroke.[15]

Backswings that go past parallel and powerful downswings that have golfers swinging from their heels have become the name of the game, especially since the likes of long-hitting John Daly and Tiger Woods have captured the public fancy (as well as a number of major-championship trophies). But swinging hard in search of the holy grail of distance is nothing new, as Jones points out in this discourse on what constitutes a powerful swing performed properly:

A tremendous amount of power can be derived from a correct use of the hips, legs, and the muscles of the back. These sources are almost entirely neglected by the average golfer who swings the club mainly with his arms. In the correct swing, the left hip leads the movement back toward the ball, generating speed and power as the unwinding progresses. At the instant of impact, the hips have turned through their positions at address, and the lower part of the body is facing almost squarely toward the hole. The unwinding of the hips culminates in a sort of wrench just before the club meets the ball, both legs combining to produce a sudden and powerful thrust up the left side of the body.[16]

Harvey Penick, the great golf teacher who included two-time Masters winner Ben Crenshaw among his mentored, had an eye for detail when it came to golf and the golf swing, and there were things he noticed about Jones that others might not have noticed had it not been pointed out to them:

Bobby's famous putter, Calamity Jane, had a lot of tape and glue on the shaft because he broke it from time to time. Calamity Jane had the loft of a two-iron, which was needed for the furry greens of those days. His putting stroke was long and smooth, like Ben Crenshaw's, but Bobby rolled the blade of the putter open and closed it during his stroke.

Like many players of the time, Bobby saw to it that his iron clubs were all red and pitted with rust on the face. This kept the ball on the face longer for more control.[17]

———

Like most great champions of any era, Jones was a crack shot with his putter, although the "never up, never in" philosophy never really factored into his putting strategy:

There is nothing—I speak from experience—in a round of either match or medal competition that bears down with quite the pressure of having continually to hole out putts of three and four feet; the kind left by overly enthusiastic approaches. For my part I have holed more long putts when trying to reach the cup with a dying ball than by "gobbling," or hitting hard. And if the dying ball touches the rim, it usually drops. And if it doesn't touch the rim—well, you can usually cover the hole and the ball with a hat, which makes your next putt simple and keeps down the strain.[18]

British author **Tom Scott,** *in the book* The Golf Immortals, *which he coauthored, saw Jones as a natural when it came to golf:*

He always struck me as an extremely natural golfer. Jones never gave any indication that he was doing anything else except obeying natural instincts. Having selected his club and given a long look at the distant target, he would walk up to the ball, fall into position apparently casually but actually with great precision, give one last look at the target and then let fly. We were not conscious, as we so often are when watching golfers today, of Jones checking up on his hands and feet, or shuffling into position with indeterminate waggles of the club. Jones seemed to arrive at the right position by instinct, or as though he were placing his feet in some depressions specially prepared for them. This was perhaps the hallmark of the born natural golfer.

I know that many fine golfers, in the past and also now, very obviously count down to their correct position. But from the moment he walked towards the ball until it was in flight, Jones pursued a rhythmic course with no jarring effect.[19]

Golfers who get nervous before any sort of golf match, whether it be a tournament or a friendly weekend game of Nassau, would have had a friend in Bobby Jones. As great a player as he

A seemingly weary Jones gets a police escort at St. Andrews, where he won the 1927 British Open for the second consecutive time. (AP/Wide World Photos)

was, Jones admits to getting the butterflies before teeing off in competition, and he suggests that it's a good thing to feel a bit nervous before a match:

I seemed to play better when nervous . . . The most unpropitious symptom I can experience before an important round, of match or medal play, is absence of nervousness. It is a rare thing for me to be able to manage even the restricted tournament breakfast, the morning on which the big show starts.

Digressing a moment, I might explain here that I play better fasting. That is one of the changes since I grew up. As a boy I loved to eat; I still love to eat, but not on the days of tournament play, until after the second round. I used to eat plenty of breakfast of my accustomed kind; oatmeal, bacon and eggs, all too frequently cakes or waffles; and coffee. And at luncheon between rounds, hungry from the exercise, I would not think of denying myself something substantial, topped off by a pie a la mode. Pie and ice cream—with an afternoon round to play!

Not any more. For breakfast, when I can eat, a strip of bacon and a small chop and a cup of black coffee. For luncheon, between rounds, a slice of dry toast and a cup of tea . . . (For tournament golf) I have a good, big dinner in my room (the night before), prefaced by two good, stiff high-balls, the first taken in a tub of hot water; the finest relaxing combination I know; and then a few cigarettes and a bit of conversation, and bed at nine o'clock. And usually I sleep well, despite the curious strain that is always present, in championship competition.[20]

Some past Masters winners more than others are closely associated with Augusta National and its showcase tournament, and **Byron Nelson** belongs to that category of legendary champions who are an integral part of Masters lore. Nelson won the Masters in 1937 and 1942 and was runner-up two other times. Nelson turned eighteen in the year that Jones won his Grand Slam in 1930 and, like other young golfers, had heard much about Jones without ever seeing him play, except for a few quick glimpses at movie theater newsreels. Jones's exploits were a source of fascination and motivation for young golfers, but that didn't necessarily carry over into copying Jones's swing as a form of emulation and idolatry. As Nelson, who grew up in the Fort Worth area in Texas, points out, up-and-coming golfers of his generation were, for the most part, self-made golfers with distinctive styles all their own:

He had already won the Grand Slam by the time I turned pro in 1932. I had read about him and heard about him, and here in Texas Bobby Jones was a great name because no one else had ever won the so-called Grand Slam like he did. Some people today haven't thought much about his Grand Slam because two of the events he won were amateur tournaments (the U.S. and British Amateurs) and two of them were professional tournaments. What these people don't realize is that back in those days, very few of the finest players turned pro because there was so little money in pro golf then. Most of the best amateurs in those days didn't turn pro because they could make a better living doing something else. So it was just as difficult to win the amateur tournaments then as it was to win the pro tournaments.

I never met Jones until I played in the Masters for the first time in 1935. I spoke to him briefly and he shook hands with me. We didn't have very many players in the tournament in those days, so he was able to greet everybody. Then in 1937, when he presented me with the championship trophy, I started to become a good friend of his. I really respected him and all that he had accomplished, although I don't think the way he played had any effect at all on the way I played golf. I had a very short, firm swing and Jones had a long, beautiful, rhythmic swing—very flowing. His swing wasn't like mine whatsoever. But you've got to remember there weren't many pictures or films in those days. Of course, he made some pictures and did some filming, one of the first golfers who ever did, but they didn't really have any effect on me.

Even when playing with other players during that time, mainly in Texas, I didn't hear any of them saying that they were doing something in their swings because they were trying to do what Jones did. But I'll tell you this, his influence on the game was great and it was because of the type of person that he was. He had a great knowledge of the game and possessed the great gift of being able to express himself about as well as anybody I ever met. Those were the kind of things he contributed that were particularly memorable. When the Masters was started, Clifford Roberts was the power behind it, but it was the Jones name and the effect he had on people because of the way they idolized him that made the tournament such an attraction right from the beginning.

So, if it wasn't Jones, who was our model golfer back then in terms of copying a great swing? Nobody. Back when we learned how to play—and I talked this over with a number of others like (Ben) Hogan, (Jimmy) Demaret, and (Jackie) Burke—and on and on—they developed their own games. Every one of us learned how to play golf by caddying. You would see how somebody swung and you tried to emulate how they swung. I know Ben had a very strong grip, which is why he hooked the ball so much in his early days. That's because the man whom he caddied for much of the time—a man by the name of Ed Stewart—played with a strong grip. That's the way you learned to play in those days. None of us ever had a lesson from anybody. You'd sometimes see a picture in a newspaper or a shot of a major tournament winner swinging in one of those newsreels that Paramount would show, but that was about it. Nowadays you hear about how everyone swings alike, when in those days no one swung alike. I had my short, firm swing with a lot of body motion, and now nobody swings like that. Everybody now sees videos and gets to see all of the other great players play. The only time I ever saw a great golfer play in person—that is, before I turned pro—was in 1927 when the pro at Glen Garden (a golf club in Fort Worth, Texas) took me over to Dallas to see Walter Hagen play in the semifinals of the PGA Championship against Al Espinosa.

I caddied for our pro when he came to try out for the job, and he had a lot of peculiarities in his swing, so he didn't do much for me in helping me with my swing. But I saw a number of good players around Fort Worth and Dallas, and that's how I learned how to play. We had no television. When I wrote my book *Winning Golf* in 1946, it had pictures in it and the pictures are fine, except there are no pictures that show the lower half of the swing. You don't see anything that happens down in the hitting area, because there was no camera made then that had the shutter speed to be able to show that properly.

***

Ask any knowledgeable golf fan to name the top players on the pro tour when it started to blossom in the 1930s and names such as Gene Sarazen and the trio of Sam Snead, Byron Nelson, and Ben Hogan quickly roll off the tongue. It just so happens that those latter three youngsters—who won a total of seven Masters titles between them—were all born within a twelve-month span in 1912 and 1913, and each discovered enough of their respective games in that decade to emerge as a new breed of star. What few golf historians can appreciate is that there was a group of other golfers who reached the apex of their careers within five years of Jones's retirement in 1930. Theirs were not household names, but they were pioneers of what came to be known as the PGA Tour. There were Horton Smith, who won two of the first three Masters Tournaments contested; Craig Wood, the 1941 Masters winner who six years earlier had been victimized when beaten in a playoff manufactured when Sarazen had scored his double eagle at Augusta's fifteenth; Henry Picard; Ralph Guldahl; Jimmy Demaret; Harry Cooper; and a young Californian by the name of **Paul Runyan,** *who was one of the top players in America during the thirties. Runyan won two PGA Championships—the only major victories of his career—and here he recalls Bobby Jones and what he brought to the game:*

Jones turned from being a brat as a youngster to a gentleman of the highest distinction later on. He certainly was the best player in the world until, in my opinion, he was surpassed by Hogan and then later by Nicklaus.

Jones was the epitome of sportsmanship and an extremely straight thinker. He was a golfer beyond compare. I got to know him quite well because in addition to being paired with him, he had played in the Augusta Open a year or two before the Masters was started, and he did something that, to me, was downright astounding: he played the last three holes of that Augusta Open in five over par and still won the tournament by a large margin over the professionals. Horton Smith got the first prize and I got the second, and that was because Jones was still playing as an amateur. I don't think he ever received prize money even after he was declared a professional because of his professional practices (which included being paid for making golf instructional films).

I didn't get to play with him in the Augusta Open, but after the Masters Tournament came along, I was the leading moneywinner and leading scorer on the pro tour. The tournament had an arrangement then whereby the leading moneywinner and leading scorer got to be paired with Jones during the first thirty-six holes of the tournament. So in that first Masters, in 1934, I had the honor of playing with him. It was a great thrill. In practice rounds, he and Ed Dudley, who was Augusta National's first resident professional, would have friendly one-dollar Nassaus against me and Horton Smith. We did this a couple of times and while Dudley contributed to their team, Jones was still the power behind that team. They beat us both times. Jones in the practice rounds was magnificent.

Jones was one of the most graceful golfers the world has ever known. MacDonald Smith and Sam Snead were among the others, too. Jones was one of the more beautiful, rhythmic golfers before or since. He was a little reticent, but he also had a great sense of humor. A very quiet sense of humor. He took his golf very seriously, being quite quiet and very orderly during the round.

In the first few years of the Masters Tournament, they had a Calcutta pool—against some people's wishes—and that pool was pretty substantial. If I remember right, Jones was always the prohibitive favorite. Like in the first tournament when the bid for me got up to around eighteen hundred dollars. I told them to stop because I didn't think I had better than a one-in-six or one-in-eight chance to win. And then the bidding on Jones got up to between twelve and thirteen thousand dollars. Obviously, that was a huge amount in those days. And I really believe that, with money being as short as it was in those days (of the Great Depression), that that was too big a load for Jones to carry on his shoulders. Being that the Masters was a straight medal-play tournament, Jones didn't have the help of Dudley as his partner in the rounds that counted, and because of that Jones never came close to winning. As a matter of fact, 72 might have been the lowest round he ever had in the playing of the Masters (it was). He never broke par. I think the fact he never played well in the Masters was largely because of that Calcutta pool. That's just my personal opinion.

———

*During his many years working the Masters as a journalist, including a lengthy stint with CBS-TV, **John Derr** had ample opportunity to sit down with Jones and talk about golf in general, not just whatever Masters Tournament action was taking place outside:*

Once at Augusta National, not at tournament time, I sat on the verandah with Jones and asked him at what point was he most nervous in a competition.

"Does it begin to get to you when you are (at) about the sixteenth hole with a lead that you don't want to slip away?" I asked.

"Oh, no. The last few holes are no time for nervousness. If you are playing well there's no need to get nervous. However, you are apt to get quicker or stronger and you have to guard against over-clubbing. Your adrenaline is so high that often you have to back off from a six- to a seven-iron.

"Nervousness? I was nervous going to the first tee in every round or every match I played in competition. I never concerned myself about the ability of others. I knew they could play, but I did wonder about my own game. You probably won't believe this, but I was nervous every time, wondering if I might whiff the ball. I was that nervous.

"My knees would be knocking, I was so unsure of what might happen on the first tee. I often wondered if people could see or hear them. If I had worn plus-fours (à la Sarazen) they could not have seen them but they might have heard them. I think they were playing 'Dixie' by the time I put the tee in the ground.

"After that first tee, no. It was done with."[21]

In between Ben Hogan's three major victories in 1953 and Tiger Woods's three in 2000, the closest anyone came to a single-season Grand Slam—what would have been the first since Jones's in 1930—was when Jack Nicklaus won the Masters and U.S. Open in 1972 before finishing second by one stroke to Lee Trevino at that year's British Open. While Nicklaus never did win the one-year Slam, he did finally surpass Jones's record of thirteen major victories. The Golden Bear tied Jones's record of thirteen by winning the 1972 Open at Pebble Beach, then surpassed the record by winning the 1973 PGA Championship at Canterbury Golf Club in Cleveland, Ohio. Nicklaus discusses his breaking Jones's lifetime major-tournament record:

Of all the records in golf, this was the one I had become the most attuned to almost from the time my dad introduced me to the game. At first it had been like the North Star—always there, always glittering, but so remote as to be forever out of reach. Them slowly but steadily year by year, it had drawn closer and closer. Now, at what must surely be the peak of my powers, I could reach out and touch it. Moreover, if my record was not a mirage, this goal, unlike the Grand Slam, was no pipe dream. If I could win thirteen major championships, there was no reason why I could not win fourteen.[22]

"Grand Slam" has long been the popular lexicon in describing the act of winning all four majors, whether it be for a career or a calendar year, but when Jones won the U.S. Amateur, U.S. Open, British Amateur, and British Open in 1930, many wags called it the "Impregnable Quadrilateral." Golf writer George Trevor was credited with that description of Jones's one-year sweep of his era's majors. **Jack Nicklaus,** *in writing about Jones in 1997, said that a one-year Slam—as defined by Jones's 1930 parameters—is an achievement that will go unmatched for eternity. That's a pretty safe bet considering that less than a handful of men have even won two of the four—the U.S. and British Opens—in the same year, and none of those—other than Jones—were amateurs. This is what Nicklaus had to say about Jones and his Grand Slam feat:*

To equal this greatest of all golfing achievements, a golfer would require two assets: supreme playing skills plus the resourcefulness and resources to remain amateur. The first of those conditions is a possibility—no, a probability. In today's world the second, to my mind, is almost a nonstarter.

In the sixty-some years since Bob's heroic achievement, golf has simply changed too much to permit even a super-humanly gifted player to win its top open-to-all championships in the same year with less than total commitment and devotion to the game—in other words, without playing professionally. Given the high and ever-rising cost of playing top tournament golf, the expense of the effort alone would be a formidable problem for an amateur not blessed with substantial private means. Should that hurdle be cleared, I believe the quantity and quality of talent at the top of golf globally would be an insuperable obstacle.

In 1930 there were perhaps ten golfers, pro or amateur,

who might defeat Jones when everything was right with them. (In fact, during his eight peak years from 1923 to 1930, he lost to only nine men in match play, and failed to win only two of the stroke-play tournaments he entered.) I

This is Jones in 1928, looking over "Calamity Jane," his famous putter. (AP/Wide World Photos)

figured standards now have risen to the point where about two-thirds of the contestants in the full-field majors—the U.S. and British Opens and the PGA—have a chance of winning, which means Bob's competition would be multiplied about tenfold . . . Most people knowledgeable about golf have shared that view, which is one of the reasons why, a decade or so after World War II, as the professional game began its first great boom period, a revised version of Bob's crowning achievement began to tickle the sportswriters' fancy, and eventually the golf fans' also. In this, the two Amateur championships were replaced by the Masters (most fittingly, it being a Bob Jones invention) and, once its playing no longer clashed with the British Open, the championship of the Professional Golfers' Association of America, better known as the PGA.[23]

Sam Snead saw Bob Jones as an unusual man when it came to the subject of golf and bulging waistlines:

A key to continue winning in the Seniors is not to let yourself get too fat. An overweight golfer, especially an older fella with less flexibility, puts on strokes whenever he puts on pounds. Bobby Jones used to like to take on a few extra pounds before he played in a championship because he felt it gave him something to burn. By the end of the tournament he'd lose all that extra weight plus some more. But Bobby Jones was an unusual man. His kind of metabolism, and self-discipline, is rare.[24]

Jack Nicklaus elaborates on the comparisons between him and Jones when it came to winning major championships. Each can claim the upper hand: Jones for his winning a one-year Grand Slam, which Nicklaus never did; and Nicklaus for his winning twenty career major titles (including his two U.S. Amateur victories) to Jones's fourteen:

In Bob Jones's day, golf's major championships consisted of four events: the U.S. and British Open and Amateur championships. Bob's thirteen victories in them comprised five U.S. Amateurs, four U.S. Opens, three British Opens, and one British Amateur. He won those championships over a period of eight years from 1923 to 1930, playing strictly as a part-timer while first obtaining three college degrees, then raising a young family and launching a career as an attorney.

The major victories credited to me at this point in my career were two U.S. Amateurs, four Masters, three U.S. Opens, two British Opens, and three PGA Championships. That is five events, not four. Had I also played each year in the British Amateur until I turned professional, my total of available majors would have become six, meaning that I enjoyed a considerably greater opportunity to win majors than Bob did. Also, even though I probably faced stiffer competition than he did, it took me from 1959 to 1973, or seven years longer than Jones, to total fourteen victories—and that while devoting as much time as I wished to golf.

Those are a few of the reasons why I felt that some of the comparisons made between Jones and me following my Canterbury win (the 1973 PGA Championship) reflected unfairly on Bob's achievements. The differences in the designation of the major championships, the differences in course and equipment quality, the differences in incentives and opportunities, and the differences in so many other areas of his time and mine are too vast to permit valid comparisons between us.[25]

Bob Goalby played a lot of golf with three-time Masters winner Sam Snead over the years, many of those being Masters practice rounds at Augusta National, and their conversation would occasionally turn to Jones as Snead regaled his younger companion with tales of Jones's exploits:

Sam told me that Jones was one guy who had two "speeds" on the par-fives. He was long. He could play the big swing and hook out there and get another twenty-five yards. That's pretty difficult for the average player to do, but he had that smooth, easy swing. Whenever he had to, he could wind it up a little bit more and hit it even harder. Snead himself said that he only ever swung at about 80 percent and that it was something he had learned from Jones. He played a few rounds with Jones in the thirties, and saw how smoothly he swung and how far he could hit it, and that helped him. Snead had that rhythmic swing anyway and maybe his seeing Jones play just cemented it.

Johnny Revolta, another veteran pro, said that Jones was a marvelous player, that he never tried to force anything. They also say he was a beautiful putter. Then again, he was playing a lot of guys who were club pros who didn't get a lot of time to play, especially those guys in the North who worked all summer and then in the winter it was too cold for them to play. They played a few events on the winter tour, but you can just imagine the kinds of courses they had to play on. Even in the late fifties, after I had started playing the tour, we didn't play one private course until we got to Augusta (in April). Sure, we did play Pebble Beach, but that was a public course, too.

Doug Ford won the 1957 Masters Tournament to solidify his status as one of his generation's better players, that coming two years after he had beaten Cary Middlecoff in the finals of the PGA Championship. Ford's victory at Augusta National gave him a lifetime ticket to the Masters, a privilege he was still taking full advantage of well into the 1990s. Decades earlier, Ford had the opportunity to see Jones in action, although that was after Jones had retired from competitive golf in 1930:

The first time I saw Jones was in an exhibition match in Connecticut when I was about ten years old. I believe he was playing with the then Open champion, Billy Burke (who won the U.S. Open in 1931, the year after Jones had completed his "Impregnable Quadrilateral"). By reputation I knew even then that he had been the best there was. My father was a golf pro and I knew enough about the swing to know to look at what he did with his swing. It was very long and very loose, what I would call the English-type swing that you finally saw fade out in the late thirties and early forties, when swings became more compact. With Jones it was a very free-flowing action. They played an eighteen-hole match, and that would have been in the early thirties. I don't think he was working much with his game at that time, and I think he was doing a favor for some charity by being there to play the exhibition.

I didn't see him again, at all, until I started to play at the Masters in '53. At that time he wasn't really crippled or anything, he was still pretty much mobile, and then to watch him each year go down so much was really sad. But he was still smiling and greeting everybody and being the perfect gentleman. It just broke your heart to see how much he was going downhill each year. He was in a lot of pain, but you would never know it. He went to the dinners and would be at some vantage points during the tournament, but that was about all.

———

Arnold Palmer was only in his early thirties when, in 1963, he started hearing whispers that he was "washed up," a major-tournament has-been no longer capable of winning one of the big events. No matter that just a little over a year earlier he had won his third Masters title at Augusta. Palmer looks back at what was being said about him in 1963 and how Jones was a part of that picture:

Although I had seven tournament victories in twenty starts that year, I failed to win any of the majors. A few people were saying that I was "washed up," perhaps ailing, undoubtedly an elder statesman of the Tour at the grand old age of thirty-four. Some said that I no longer had the incentive to play like the Palmer of yesterday, and it didn't help my mood a bit that Bob Jones, when asked by a reporter to comment on my "major" drought, said that the so-called Palmer Era could be over—if it ever existed anyway. Jones wasn't trying to be unkind; he was merely describing what he thought he saw. So was Pap when he sharply observed to a reporter who had asked more or less the same question as the one posed to Mr. Jones. "There's nothing wrong with Arnie's game—he just has too many irons in the fire. He's got to decide whether he wants to play golf or make television films with Bob Hope. With this boy Nicklaus coming along the way he is, Arnie can't do both."[26]

Atlantan **Tommy Barnes** *recalls a couple of Jones stories told to him by Jones's friend and ghostwriter O. B. Keeler, with whom Barnes and fellow Atlanta amateur star Charlie Yates spent ten nights in 1937 in a Pullman traveling ten thousand miles for the U.S. Amateur in Portland, Oregon, followed by the Western Amateur in Los Angeles, followed by a cross-country trek back that took them through New Orleans:*

I remember coming in from a round of golf (at East Lake) and telling O. B., "I think I'll go take a swim now," and O.B. would say, "Bob never did." If there ever was anything O. B. didn't want you to do, he would say, "Bob never did."

There's another story he told about the National Amateur one time where this one golfer had an almost impossible shot around a big tree, and Bob Jones, O. B., and some other fellows were standing there watching this, and the guy hit the ball right around that tree and onto the green, at which point Bob said, "That's the most fantastic shot I've ever seen played in golf. I don't think anybody else could have played that shot." An older gentleman standing nearby watching all this said, "I beg to differ with you, mister."

And Jones said, "What do you mean?"

And the guy said, "Well, I know another guy who could do it."

"Who's that?"

"Bob Jones."

"Nah, I don't think he could do that."

"You don't? Did you ever see that S.O.B. play?"

Bob never said anything after that. He didn't even let on that he was Bob Jones.

Although golfer **Paul Runyan** *got to make his acquaintance with Jones as a Masters contestant and as one of the top players of that era, he didn't really get to know Jones until after he had trimmed back his playing schedule to go on the road working as a representative for Spalding. One of the benefits of the position was that Atlanta was in his territory and that afforded him the chance to drop in on Jones at Jones's Atlanta office over the years. As Runyan remembers it, Jones was always accommodating and a good conversationalist during these meetings:*

Spalding sent me to Atlanta for several years to help sell their equipment through Rich's Department Store. It was located only a few blocks from Jones's office. And he invited me to his office secretly to talk about golf and particularly the Masters. Those visits with him were always something. I saw him five or six times during those visits, and they would last an hour or an hour and a half. We discussed many other things as well. By this time, his health was deteriorating rapidly.

The first time I went to see him on one of those visits, he was still healthy and still a wonderful golfer. He played very well. But in the latter years of the Masters before his death, he was traveling around the golf course in his electric cart. When I went to see him at his offices, each time I saw him I liked him more and more, and realized more and more just how much of an asset he had been to golf in general, as had Walter Hagen. Jones maybe had even more of a role in promoting the popularity of golf. He even got to where he would discuss with me his early days learning golf from Stewart Maiden and his days growing up at East Lake Country Club in Atlanta.

We would always get around to discussing Horton Smith a little bit. Horton was one of those unusual people who didn't think with his heart, he thought with his head. When he was talking with Jones, the conversation usually just went over my head. Horton was president of the PGA, and before he became president, I got the impression the PGA was a fraternal organization and he changed it into a business organization. That's a big difference.

As Augusta National's official photographer for many years, **Frank Christian Jr.** *had tremendous access to the likes of Bobby Jones, and he benefited from that fairly close association by getting to know Jones quite well on a personal level:*

I went out and photographed him during what I think was the last time he played Augusta National. He played with a few friends, and I didn't know it was the last round he was going to play there.

He was always amazing to watch. He didn't play very well the last few years he did play, and I think that was very frustrating for him because I'm sure he didn't like playing substandard to what he was used to. I then went away for a time in the fifties to be in the air force and when I came back I could see that he was ill. He did come out for special occasions such as the gathering for the Jamboree and, of course, the Masters Tournament, but he was very scarce from those times on because of a very debilitating disease that made it very uncomfortable for him.

The one thing that sticks in my mind was how always gracious he was. He was just head and shoulders over all men, and many were attracted to him because he was their hero; he was what most of them wanted to be. He was just always a pleasure to be around. I know he used to love to smoke his cigar. One of my favorite photos of him is one showing him sitting on the grass with his legs folded underneath him and a big stogie in his mouth. In fact I've got several photos of him made in the locker room where he's sitting down puffing away on a big cigar.

Even long after he retired from competitive golf, he could do some amazing things with a golf club in hand. I remember one time when I was a young kid and my father took me over to the club. We had a little group of kids from our grammar school. And Bobby Jones came out to see us and to give a little demonstration on how to hold a golf club and how to chip, stuff like that. He then took a matchbox out of his pocket, emptied out the matches, and placed the box a little ways away on the grass. This wasn't out on the golf course, we were just out in front of the club. He then grabbed a pitching wedge and a few golf balls and started chipping. He put the first one right into the little matchbox, and it hopped out. He then put the second one into the box and then the third. It was incredible. As young kids watching this, we figured this was what you were supposed to be able to do all the time, and of course we now know just how difficult that must have been. That was some kind of demonstration. He must have been about fourteen or fifteen feet away.

Later on I remember watching the instructional films that he made, and there was one in particular where he was demonstrating the three-wood. He dropped three balls and, one after another, he hit them all to within about five feet of the pin. Then he showed how sometimes you had to play a bank shot off of a tree because of the ball's lie, and he demonstrated how to do it by putting several shots like that right next to the hole. That's one other reason why he was so great in his day. He could take any difficult shot and create an effective solution.

———

Jones sincerely enjoyed the many recreational rounds of golf he played with friends, and he went out of his way to show that he cared as much about his partners' enjoyment of the game as he did his own, as veteran golf journalist **John Derr** *found out, which he wrote about in his book* Uphill Is Easier:

It was my pleasure to play in a four-ball with Bob several times, at Augusta and elsewhere. Usually it was as a result of someone having to cancel unexpectedly and I would fill in.

Our last game I remember best. It was in November 1944. We played at East Lake in Atlanta, Bob's home course there. Tar Heel Johnny Bulla, a talented ambidextrous professional, arranged the game. He and I opposed Jones and a good amateur friend of his, Charlie White.

I lost a ball in the woods to the right of the fairway on an early hole. The leaves had started to fall and we had trouble spotting the ball. One of life's most embarrassing moments came when during the search I looked up and saw the great Bob Jones, practically on his hands and knees, brushing aside the oak leaves . . . looking for my ball.

Jones played well that day, despite the distractions. He scored 70, two under. I later learned this was probably the last time he broke par at his home course. White played well, too, 71.

But we won.

I wish I had saved those four dollar bills Jones paid me that day. I should have had them framed, but I was still in the service and they amounted to folding money then.

Oh, I told you Jones broke par with 70. Did I mention that Bulla broke par, too? Johnny had a 66. My score was an unremarkable 84 . . . but we won from Bob Jones on his home course . . . with a little help.

Bulla, an old friend from Greensboro, was not only a professional golfer who could play as well left-handed as right-handed, but he was a commercial airline pilot and also known as a competent hypnotist. That day when we had showered and dressed, Jones was asking Bulla about the time he'd hypnotized Snead.

"Would you like to see me hypnotize John?" Bulla asked.

Jones said he would, and since Bulla had cast his spell over me previously, I was not afraid to undergo his hypnosis. After all, you don't have to be a rocket scientist to be an acceptable hypnosis subject.

Under Bulla's mystical persuasion I am told he had me do several minor exercises and while still under his control he told me that Jones was wearing his (Bulla's) necktie. He would probably try to leave the club still wearing it.

The tie had to be recovered. No matter how much Jones protested, I was to insist on getting back Bulla's tie.

Jones started for the door. I kindly suggested he remove Bulla's tie. Jones claimed it was his. Bulla again told me to get the tie, not to let him leave the locker room wearing it.

Having no success through pleading, I proceeded to back Jones up to the wall. Now, if necessary, I would physically remove it.

Just before the mayhem was committed, Bulla snapped his fingers and brought me from hypnosis.

"It's all right," Bulla said, "just a little misunderstanding. Let him go."

What a shocker, to come out of hypnosis when your hands are around the throat of the greatest golfer who ever lived. I had really tried to follow orders. Jones swore his neck was sore for a week.[27]

3

AUGUSTA AND THE MASTERS

It wasn't by chance that Jones picked Augusta as the home site for what would be his dream golf club and course. Otherwise a plantation and mill town, Augusta by the early 1900s had become known as a popular resort destination for travelers and vacationers who wanted to experience some of the enduring ambiance of the Old South. The many stately homes of Augusta were proof that this was more than just a small, quaint town of fifty thousand people, and the attendant warm climate and lush flora proved irresistible to many. Among those who often made the trip to the small city just off the South Carolina border were "Colonel" Bob Jones and his family, including young Bobby.

Augusta was no stranger to great golf, either. Even before Augusta National was erected on a 365-acre site that had been a tree nursery, called "the Fruitlands," it had become known as a winter golf haven boasting two Donald Ross–designed golf courses. By 1928, Jones was already contemplating retirement from competitive golf and envisioning his baby, a golf club where he and his friends could congregate in private and play golf, socialize, drink, smoke, and laugh. By the time Jones retired in 1930, the country had entered the Great Depression, and even with Wall Street whiz Clifford Roberts joining Jones to round up investors, it was a struggle to get all the financing needed to complete construction of a course. Enough money ultimately came through, the course was completed under the direction of architect Alister Mackenzie with Jones's assistance, and Augusta National was opened for play in 1933.

A year later Jones and Roberts launched an annual Augusta invitational that would become known as the Masters Tournament and feature many of the great names in golf. Horton Smith won the first Masters, in 1934, and a year later Gene Sarazen scored the memorable double eagle at fifteen that inspired his eventual playoff victory over Craig Wood. Sarazen's dramatic victory gave Augusta and the Masters the first big boost toward becoming one of the most prestigious sporting events in the world, perhaps comparable in prestige and intrigue to the likes of the Super Bowl, the World Cup, the Olympics, and the World Series. Jones never won his own tournament, and in fact he never broke par in a Masters round, but his close association with the event was instrumental in making the Masters and Augusta crown jewels in America's sporting landscape.

Clifford Roberts was the savvy Wall Street investor who teamed up with Jones to create Augusta National Golf Club and the tournament that soon came to be known as the Masters.

Theirs was perhaps the most significant relationship in American golf history and in discussing Augusta National and the Masters, it is almost impossible to speak a paragraph about one of the men without mentioning the other. They had not been childhood friends; they didn't meet until their adult years, and other than the business of golf, there really wasn't much about either man to suggest one would have been at all compatible with the other in a social setting.

Jones and Roberts weren't exactly oil and water—they did mix, and somehow they mixed well, perhaps as complementing parts that allowed them to achieve much more as a whole than the sum of their parts. Both had their share of friends, although Roberts probably could have counted his on one hand—okay, maybe he would have needed the other, too—whereas anyone who met Jones and spent any time with him would quickly think of him as a friend. Not that Jones was gregarious in any sort of way; he wasn't. But his door seemed to be open to others more than Roberts's was. If Jones could be described as gracious, Roberts would counter with rigidity. Roberts was a buttoned-down, tightfisted money man who understood the power of political influence behind the scenes, while Jones was the consummate gentleman golfer always open to a friendly game of golf yet keeping the game in perspective. There was more to him than life at Augusta, as Atlanta remained his true home until his death in 1971.

One possible analogy of the Roberts-Jones relationship would be of fight trainer and champion boxer. Roberts was the businessman who astutely understood the value of Jones's golf legacy and knew how to send Jones into the ring prepared, while Jones was the popular champion, his name proving to be the drawing card Augusta National needed in laying its seeds for future greatness. What Roberts didn't know about golf, he learned from Bobby Jones; and what Jones didn't know about the business of building and then running a business—a golf club—he learned from Roberts. They probably weren't close, warm friends, but for decades they had a powerful admiration for one another, and together they formed a dynamic team that turned Augusta, Georgia, into the capital of golf in America.

This is how Roberts remembered Jones:

I would describe Bob in his twenties as a quite handsome young athlete who seemed at the same time very manly. He had an engaging smile, but this did not prevent his looking squarely at the person to whom he was being introduced. His handshake was firm and his attitude quite friendly. He somehow managed to give everyone the impression that he was genuinely pleased about the introduction. Not once did I ever hear a person classify Bob as a bored celebrity.[1]

Creating Augusta National Golf Club was not a simple task for Roberts and Jones. They almost didn't succeed. This was the early 1930s and America was in the throes of the Great Depression. But this was to be the realization of a dream for Jones—the consummate golf club where he and friends could gather to play golf on a heavenly golf course and enjoy their camaraderie smoking stogies, playing cards, or enjoying fine Southern cuisine, perhaps with a glass of fine wine or some other spirits a tad stronger. Jones, Roberts, and several cronies pooled $70,000 to buy the 365-acre Fruitlands tract from the Berckman family, but even then it was a struggle, as **Roberts** pointed out, to find enough other investors—i.e., members—to take the club from the drawing board to actuality:

Bob Jones took the position that he wold not ask anyone in Atlanta to help finance his project in Augusta, and urged me not to do anything other than take what was offered by Atlanta. While he never complained about it, I knew he was keenly disappointed that only one of his Atlanta friends became an underwriter, which may have been one of the reasons why he volunteered on several occasions later to contribute five thousand dollars or more to the club.[2]

—————

To know the Augusta National golf course, even with all of its tweaks and adjustments over the years, is to know a little bit about Bobby Jones and what kind of golfer he was—his strengths, his weaknesses, and his criteria for testing golfers without discouraging them. Former PGA Tour pro **Lionel Hebert** *played in more than a dozen Masters Tournaments, and that gave him a good feel for Jones, the golfer:*

He built (along with noted architect Dr. Alister Mackenzie) that golf course as tough as he could build it and as chancy as he could build it, for that time. In other words, Jones probably never envisioned that there would be a guy who could hit the ball 350 yards off the tee. Now they're building golf courses longer and harder, sometimes forgetting that the average golfer is the one spending the money and is the one who keeps things going. Your great golfers spend hardly anything (to play). Think about it.

Augusta's been rebuilt something like 150 times, even if just one fairway at a time, or one tree at a time, or one green at a time. There have been a number of holes that have been lengthened, although there isn't much room to lengthen the golf course.

The whole thing is, he (Jones) built the golf course and started the golf tournament. He and Mr. Roberts had a set of rules and that's the way it was. You can belong to the club, but as far as I know, you can't become a stockholding member. They have strict, exacting regulations even down to the fact that when you were a contestant there, they only allowed you a certain number of passes, and you had to order them and you had to pay for them. Jones said, "If you gave them more than that, people will be on your back all the time." That's fifty years ago. This is a guy who knew. He knew what the tournament would come to.

As far as Jones as a golfer, I knew he had a temper just from watching some of the films of him I saw. But hell, you show me a golfer who doesn't have a bad temper, and I'll show you a golfer that is a bad competitor. I've been a golf pro since 1950 and have known all the guys from the thirties on. I played golf with "the Squire," Gene Sarazen, and then there's Paul Runyan. He always looked at Jay (Hebert) and me as old friends. I've been blessed and Jay was blessed that these old-timers liked us. I knew Jones pretty well from a distance, but I didn't get to socialize with him much. When I went to Augusta, I went there to work and I never got to go to any of those suppers (Champions Dinners) because I never won the tournament. I had a chance to win it a couple of times, but blew it on one hole each time.

—————

Byron Nelson remembers the early days of the Masters as something quite special, long before television had helped turn it into an annual sports spectacle beamed to all corners of the world:

The feel of the tournament was premised on the fact that Bobby Jones was there, as was Magnolia Avenue and a little clubhouse that was the center of everything that took place—just a nice little building. You were assigned a caddie and then you went to play. The course was a lot different then because of all the minor and major changes that they have made to it since. Jones was the master of ceremonies. There already was a nostalgia built in to the tournament because the name of Jones was so big. That helped get it started. Then add to the fact that Clifford Roberts was such a perfectionist.

Jones's name was the main draw, but they started right off with a strict set of rules such as not allowing players practicing for the Masters to hit extra balls to the green or to practice hitting putts on the greens. So right from the beginning they set out to do the right things and laid the seeds for it to grow into something special, and those seeds grew very, very quickly. When I won the Masters in 1937 (the fourth time the tournament was played) it put me on the Ryder Cup team, which tells you just how quickly the Masters became such a big tournament with so much prestige.

Popular sentiment at Augusta National has been a result of revisionist history of sorts, in that Jones is often credited as the person who had control over the design of the National's golf course. Jones was involved in the design and his stamp is evident in the layout even today, although let's not forget that it was the great

*Scottish designer, Dr. Alister Mackenzie, who spearheaded the
design of the course, modeled in part after California's Cypress
Point, which also had been Mackenzie's handiwork. Two-time
Masters winner* **Byron Nelson** *puts all this into some perspective:*

Let's say that Jones helped Mackenzie (and not the other
way around). Originally, it reflected the kind of golfer Jones
was and what he liked and didn't like about golf course
design. A lot of that carried through until just recently. Jones
didn't like rough; he didn't believe in rough. But he did
believe that if you were on the wrong side of the green, you
would have a difficult job two-putting. And if you were on
the wrong side of the fairway, with the way the greens were
set, you would have a very difficult approach shot.

I remember that time when someone complained about
the pin setting at the third hole, saying it made it too difficult to birdie the hole, and Jones countered by asking,
rhetorically, why golfers felt they needed to be able to birdie
every hole. When you put the pin in back of the third green
on the left side, you couldn't shoot at that pin and stay on
the green. You had to play to the right of the pin and let the
ball filter down toward the hole, sort of curving to the left.
And pros being pros, we would often complain about holes
that were set up in such a way as to make it hard to make a
birdie. Finally, Jones said, "You're not always supposed to
shoot at the flag. You should also be able to, when necessary,
shoot at the other side of the green and even play it something like a pitch and run where you can spin it back over to
the side of the green where the hole is." That's the way the
greens at Augusta National were designed.

Of course, their greens were very hard in those days. On
some of the holes you had to be able to play a low shot that

would run up and onto the greens. That's why that course became known as so great early on because those were the kinds of shots that you sometimes had to play. But nobody who hit the ball low all the time was going to win at Augusta. You had to be able to get the ball into the air. That's one reason (Jack) Nicklaus was so great at Augusta. He always hit the ball so nice and high. He was also the greatest fast-green putter I've ever seen. (Lee) Trevino never won at Augusta, he said, because he always played a fade and he would say, "I can never win at Augusta because you have to be able to hook the ball there." Well, I never hooked the ball and I won twice there. And Jimmy Demaret won it three times and he faded the ball, too.

Photographer **Frank Christian Jr.** *continued a family legacy when he assumed from his father Frank Sr. the position of official photographer at Augusta National Golf Club. Young Frank was born a year after the first Masters Tournament, then called an Invitational, was played, but through his father's work at the club he was able to meet and befriend Bobby Jones at an early age. Christian fills us in with some background as he recalls his early meetings with and impressions of the venerable Jones:*

My father came to Augusta from Pittsburgh in 1927 to work for his uncle Montell, who was a very famous photographer at the time. When my father got there that summer, my great-uncle gave him a camera and said, "Go out and learn how to shoot pictures." The Forest Hills club had just opened at the time, and Bobby Jones used to love to come down and play there. My father would go out to Forest Hills and walk around with his camera and catch people playing golf, riding horses, swimming, or whatever, and he would stop them and take their photograph. He would go home that evening and process the film, and then the next day he would go back with fresh pictures and more film and try to get the guests to purchase the pictures he had made the previous day. It's called "kidnapping."

My dad got to meet Mr. Jones through that. As a matter of fact, in 1930 my father got to cover the Southeastern Open. They eventually became friends, and when Bobby Jones and Clifford Roberts decided to start up Augusta National a few years later, he asked my father to come along to be the club photographer, which he did. That's what he ended up doing for most of his life until he had a heart attack and retired. I started working for my father at Augusta National and the first photos I made professionally were for the newspaper in 1948. I had met Bob Jones in around 1940 or 1941, and he gave me a driving club while also showing me how to hold it and how to swing it. I took it home and would hit anything I could find to hit with it, to include rocks and tennis balls.

Bob Jones was a wonderful man. He had a way about him that I've never seen anyone else use. When he talked to you, he looked directly at you and didn't seem to be bothered by anything else that might be going on around him. Any time I saw him he would always take the time to show interest by asking questions about school, how I was getting along, my golf game—those sorts of things. I don't know of anyone who ever met him that didn't love him. He had a very soft-spoken voice. He was a very bright person and had a great command of the English language.

Charlie Yates is one of the few Georgians still alive at the writing of this book who could say that he not only knew Jones personally, but he also had the pleasure and privilege of playing golf with and against Jones. Yates and his brother, Dan, spent many years as mainstays in the pressroom during Masters Tournament week at Augusta National Golf Club. This story, told by Charlie Yates, makes reference to the Jamboree, an annual members-guests tournament at Augusta National:

There was one story that Bob always used to tell, and it became a tradition to call on him to tell it. It concerned a new member of the club who was a nervous sort of fellow. He was attending his first Jamboree, and after dinner he got involved in a bridge game that deteriorated into poker. To settle his nerves, he was drinking pretty steadily, and when they finally poured him into bed, at three o'clock in the morning, he was as drunk as a hoot owl.

Well, at eight o'clock they awakened him and took him out to the first tee. This fellow had a handicap of eighteen, a stroke a hole, and he was paired with a fellow who had a handicap that was much lower. On the first tee, the low-handicap fellow sliced his ball so far that it hasn't been found yet. Now, our hero, who was about to jump out of his skin, stepped up on the tee and topped his drive down the hill. The ground was hard, and it rolled to the bottom. When he got to it, his caddie gave him a spoon—and he topped it again. But the ball bounced along and bounced along past that trap on the right side of the fairway, and it rolled up to where he had about 125 yards to the green. He said to his caddie, "What should I use now?" And the caddie said, "Oh, just go ahead and use the one you've got—it doesn't make any difference." Well, he topped the ball a third time. The pin was cut over there on the left, behind that trap. The ball rolled up the front of the green, just missing the trap, and stopped about six feet from the hole.

So here was our hero with a six-foot putt for par, which would be a net birdie, and his partner was in his pocket. When he stood up to the ball, his hands were shaking on his putter. They kept shaking and he took the putter back. Then, just as he stroked the ball, a great big collie dog came running up from somewhere, and it ran between his legs. Miraculously, though, the ball went into the hole, and the low-handicap fellow rushed up and said, "Partner, that's the greatest display of coolness and calmness under fire I've ever seen. How in the hell did you make that putt when that collie dog was running right between your legs?" And the fellow said, "My God—was that a real dog?"[3]

———

*Financial issues aside, **Roberts** saw in Jones an accomplished golf champion with a dream that went beyond a simple trophy. It would be a golf club and course designed in his own image, and it would be a great creation that Roberts would do anything he could to help make possible:*

Bob Jones had planned for some years to build a golf course to his own liking. It was a creative instinct on his part.

In playing various courses, Bob had become a student of golf course architecture and was eager to try his hand at it. His idea was to utilize the natural advantages of the property that might be selected, rather than to impose any particular type of golf hole which might result in artificiality rather than the natural-made layout he had in mind. He wanted particularly to avoid precipitous slopes, which are artificial in appearance and expensive to maintain. He planned to use mounds rather than too many bunkers, on the theory that they are more pleasing in appearance, require less upkeep, and can be quite effective as hazards. He hoped to find a mildly rolling piece of ground with a creek or two that could provide some lateral water hazards. His chief objective was an interesting course that would be popular with the dues-paying members.[4]

—————

By demonstrating that it was possible for a golfer to make good money playing golf in America, and to do so in grand style in front of largely appreciative audiences, **Walter Hagen** *paved the way for golfers coming into the game behind him. Jones would have been the obvious pick as Hagen's successor of the king of pros in America, but Jones retired from the game in 1930 before ever turning professional. Instead, Jones set his sights on a law career in Atlanta while working with Clifford Roberts to create the Augusta National Golf Club, where the first tournament that would a few years later come to be known as the Masters was contested. Thanks to a confluence of Hagen's paving the way for pro golfers and the creation of Augusta National and the Masters, a new breed of golfer quickly emerged—golfers willing to scratch out a living, often carpooling while traveling around the country to play on a bur-geoning tour that eventually came to be known as the PGA Tour:*

One of those early nomads in the game was Byron Nelson, the lean, soft-spoken Texan who in 1945 would set a record

As great a champion as Jones was, he never won his own Masters Tournament. In fact, he never broke par in any Masters round. Here he is in 1937 at the third hole at Augusta making his third of four putts at the treacherous third green. (AP/Wide World Photos)

in golf that likely will never be broken—eighteen victories in one year, including eleven in a row. But that sterling year of 1945 is not what put Nelson on the map, so to speak. His big breakthrough had come in 1937, when he won the Masters Tournament at Augusta, and that victory propelled Nelson into the inner circle of great golfers who were able to call Jones a friend. In looking back on his association with Jones, Nelson offers memories as fresh to him today as they were sixty or more years ago:

He was a wonderful man, with great knowledge about the history of the game and the best way to play. His ability to judge players and know what they needed to do to play good golf was excellent. . . .

I was fortunate to have played with Bob a number of times at Augusta and always enjoyed it very much. You felt an awe when you played with him, regardless of what kind of game you played yourself. His attitude toward everyone was very friendly, but he was kind of quiet, really, and didn't have a lot to say most of the time. One time at the Masters Club dinner—the one attended originally just by the Masters winner plus Bob Jones and Clifford Roberts—the players were criticizing the way the pin had been placed on the third hole because it was nearly impossible to make a birdie. All of a sudden Jones said, "You guys make me sick. You think you've got to birdie every hole. You birdie a lot of them as it is, and there are going to be some tough pin placements out there that if you want a birdie, you're really going to have to earn it."

One of the great honors of my career was when Jones asked me to play in his place with the Masters Tournament leader the last round, which I did until Ken Venturi was the leader in 1956. Since I was Venturi's mentor, Cliff and Bob decided that it wouldn't be right for me to play with Kenny, so they put me with someone else, and Kenny played with Snead and lost. From then on, they began pairing the players according to their score only, which was really the best way.[5]

The early days of the Masters were actually the beginning of the end of another era in Augusta, Georgia, which had long been a popular albeit sleepy vacation destination for travelers, many of whom migrated to the Bon Air Vanderbilt Hotel, which was a popular resort for golfers as well as vacationers. **Freddie Haas's** *history at Augusta goes back far enough for him to remember those days of yesteryear, much of which is no longer a part of the Augusta culture:*

Charlie Yates and I roomed for a year or two when we played there instead of spending fifteen or twenty dollars a day to stay at the Bon Air Vanderbilt. We had a room with two big beds in it for six dollars apiece for the week. Of course, we spent all our free time at the Bon Air Vanderbilt, where they had things like free lunches and hors d'oeuvres. It worked out pretty good.

The Masters didn't really become a big tournament in the sense it is regarded today until television came along. After television came along, Arnold Palmer stepped into the picture, and he pulled off some heroics that were memorable and kind of made the tournament. It really brought golf to people who hadn't given much thought to it before. It was one of the real big events in the history of golf. But in the early years of the Masters, there was a problem with the PGA. The PGA wanted to run all of its tournaments, and the Masters wanted to run their tournament their own way. George Snider, bless his heart, the tournament director of the PGA, somehow got the idea that one way or another the Masters should be under the wing of the PGA. George said to the fellows, "Let's get an understanding with the Masters that the Masters is going to let the PGA run the tournament." Horton Smith was the president of the association at the time, and I told him, "Horton, there are a lot of people that think the PGA ought to run this tournament; frankly, I don't. I think they have shown they can do this tournament up really good on their own and I think we ought to stay right where we are. But things might happen." And he said,

"I've heard rumors about that, but I'm not playing on the tour anymore, so I don't know exactly what's going on." I said, "To me, the tournament already is a success, and I don't think you ought to tamper with their success. This is something special."

There was some sort of vote taken, and I don't think it was an official vote, but the consensus of opinion seemed to be that the PGA pros would no longer play in the Masters anymore unless it was under the auspices of the PGA. Well, when that broke at the Masters, Horton said, "I've got to do something about this." So what did he do? He fired George Snider right on the spot. Then he looked every player in the eye. He didn't need to say anything. Not one player came out in support of George to say that he wouldn't play in the Masters. Not one, even though before there had been indications that quite a few wouldn't play.

Neither Cliff Roberts nor Bobby Jones had anything to do with any of this at all. It was Horton Smith who took care of the PGA players himself. He said, "Mr. Snider, we no longer need your services. Goodbye." As soon as he left, the players didn't have anyone else to support. All of a sudden there was a quiet and nothing else was said about it. Someone else was named tournament director. To tell you the truth, it was almost like a hush-hush deal. But it happened.

——————

Although Jones was reasonably accessible during Masters week, he was not what you would call an outgoing host. He didn't "work the room," and wasn't one to be doing a lot of backslapping. That wasn't his style. All told, he played in twelve

*Masters Tournaments without ever contending, and he did
retain a reasonably high degree of visibility for a few years after
he stopped playing in the tournament, but as time went on and
after he became ill, he became a near-recluse during Masters
week.* **Freddie Haas** *remembers what it was like and how
things changed over the years:*

Jones was there, early on as a contestant, then as a spectator
before he became an invalid. He didn't go around greeting
everyone when they came to Augusta for Masters week;
everybody went up to him. It was our pleasure, the players'
pleasure, to go over to him and tell him what an honor it was
to play in the tournament. It was so nice of him to be putting
the tournament on. Bobby didn't have the time to go see the
people, but they took the time to go see him. And his partner, Clifford Roberts, was outstanding in running the tournament. Jones was a dominating figure, no question about it.

Paul Runyan, *one of the game's top players in the thirties,
never won the Masters, but he was an integral part of Masters
week from its beginnings in 1934. Runyan reminisces about the
tournament in those early days and what the allure of Bobby
Jones was all about:*

Even in its early years it was something special. The purse for
the tournament was five thousand dollars, I think, and that
was pretty good for those days and it went up to something
like seven or eight thousand dollars within the first two or
three years. It was something special because of Jones and
because of Clifford Roberts, and because they had taken that

old (tree) nursery and made it into a magnificent golf course right from the very first. It was magnificent even in those days and has been improved since then, and lengthened. But it still hasn't really been changed from its original beauty.

Right from the very beginning of Augusta National and the Masters, Jones and Roberts conceived something that would be very wonderful, and they ran it very well. They invited all of the champions of the world, and while not all of them came, a good many did. In the early days, some of the Oriental nations—their champions weren't high-class yet; a lot of them shot in the 80s—would come over and play in the Masters. This very concept of being so inclusive was something special.

No one knows better just how photogenic Augusta National is than longtime club photographer **Frank Christian Jr.,** *who was born in 1935 and essentially grew up at the club, first as an apprentice for his father then as the club's head photographer. Christian is intimately familiar with about every nook, cranny, and undulation at Augusta, and he has long seen a course that reflects the personality of Bobby Jones, who assisted legendary architect Dr. Alister Mackenzie in the design of the course:*

Jones made some comments when he laid out the golf course, with some help from Alister Mackenzie, that he wanted it to reward the good golfer and penalize a shot gone bad. From the front tees, it's a fun course for the average golfer. You've got to remember that the average age of the members has to be in the seventies, and therefore all these heads of corporations and companies don't want to be challenged too much in playing the course because they have enough challenges as it is back in the corporate world. They've only got something like forty-three or forty-four bunkers, so it's not that difficult a golf course.

When he was helping to lay it out, Jones had certain ideas in mind because he had been all over the world playing a variety of golf courses, and I think he designed some of the holes based on some of the ones he had played in other parts of the world. But he didn't want to disturb the land much, preferring the course as it lay. I remember looking at a lot of the photos that my father made when they were building the course, and included was even a photo my dad had made of the first trees being cut down. They used mules for much of the heavy work that had to be done, but they didn't move much land, except where they had some problems with water and water runoff, which is something that has had to be fixed a number of times over the years.

You wonder today when you see this most magnificent, manicured course if this is the course that Jones had in mind when it was being built. I am reminded of the famous landscape architect Lancelot "Capability" Brown, who had designed many of the great gardens in Europe with an eye for knowing what they would look like a hundred years from now, when they were fully grown. I think that's kind of what Jones had in mind knowing that this had been a (tree) nursery and that the Berckmans (the family that sold the land to Jones et al.) had planted many trees and shrubs from all over the world. It had that aspect of already being developed. But if you look at the photographs taken when Augusta was being built, many of the trees were very small.

The most significant changes I remember were on number ten and then, about 1947, Robert Trent Jones came in and changed number sixteen (a par-three over water) to make it what it is today—many tournaments are won or lost right there. You've seen it happen. I think Jones was envisioning things a hundred or two hundred years later.

—⟨⟩—

Roberts *released the following Masters-related statement to the press on February 14, 1949, following surgery on Jones. This was one of the first early signs that there was something seriously wrong with Jones, and for the next twenty-two years the great golf champion would quietly suffer in agony while continuing to nurture a club and tournament that became American institutions:*

Mr. Robert T. Jones Jr., our president, will not participate this year as a contestant. I think it is proper to state frankly to Bob's friends that his operation was quite serious but that a complete recovery is expected. As the result of an injury to the upper part of the spine, which is believed by his doctors to have occurred when he was quite young, Bob has occasionally suffered, for some years, from what he called a "crick" in his neck and a lame shoulder. The first noticeable discomfort occurred in Scotland in 1926, but the exact cause of the trouble was never accurately determined until 1948. (The condition never interrupted tournament play except on one occasion—the 1940 Masters Tournament.) The operation was to relieve pressure on the spinal cord, which pressure had, during last year, seriously affected his central nervous system. He has not as yet regained the full use of his right leg but otherwise is in excellent health. He has already visited the Augusta National once this season and will be present during the Masters. Moreover, Bob plans to lend a hand in the directing of the tournament, something that his nonplaying status leaves him free to do.[6]

———————

Clifford Roberts describes how Jones made every effort to remain an active part of the activities during Masters Tournament week, even after Jones's illness was clearly sending Jones on a downhill slide that would last more than twenty years:

When Bob Jones first became lame he could himself still operate a golf cart. By this means he was able for some years to see something of each Masters Tournament. As he lost strength in his arms, as well as in his legs, someone would do the driving for him, with Bob strapped to his seat. His mind was never adversely affected, and he participated in the deliberations of the tournament rules committee when difficult decisions needed to be rendered. Bob chiefly officiated at the presentation ceremony at the conclusion of each tournament. His inimitable style, and his wonderfully well-worded tribute to the winner and the runners-up, put him in a class all by himself as a master of ceremonies.[7]

———————

In 1966 Augusta National Golf Club adopted the following resolution in honor of Jones, who was five years away from his death following a long illness:

It has been well and truly said that "Every great institution is the lengthened shadow of a man." So it is with the Augusta

National Golf Club: the man being Robert Tyre Jones Jr.

His was the established and unique leadership position coupled with remarkable ability, which was principally responsible for the organization and development of the Augusta National Golf Club and the Masters Tournament. He exemplifies the highest standards of sportsmanship and his position is pre-eminent throughout and beyond the golfing world.

Bob Jones, as he is affectionately known to his fellow members, has served as President of the Augusta National Golf Club from its very beginning, being unanimously elected each succeeding year, and it is desired that the distinction of being the only President of the Club be preserved by changing the By-Laws so as to provide for his election as President in Perpetuity. More especially, it is desired that the spirit of his principles, his acts of good sportsmanship, his innate modesty, and other admirable and lovable qualities shall forever guide the policies of the Augusta National and the Masters Tournament.

NOW, THEREFORE, BE IT RESOLVED, That the By-Laws be amended to provide for the position of a President in Perpetuity as a lasting tribute to Robert Tyre Jones, Jr., and that he be the only person ever to be elected to that position.

Resolved, further, That the name of Robert Tyre Jones Jr., President in Perpetuity, be carried on the letterhead and masthead of the Augusta National Golf Club as long as it continues in existence.

John Derr, longtime golf journalist and former CBS-TV golf announcer, gives the following history lesson in how television coverage was set up for the Masters in the early days, with the guiding hand of Jones:

In 1955 we had bought the rights, and our first telecast of the Masters was to be in 1956. In the fall of 1955 our CBS producer, our engineers, and I went down to Augusta to determine where we were going to put the cameras. They had provided us with a station wagon and we had a chauffeur driving it. Mr. Jones offered to help us determine where the cameras would be located. They had never had television there, and they were a little afraid of it, not knowing what it might do to their attendance. Little did they know that it would bring crowds of people wanting to get in. That first year of television we had to black out everything from Charlotte to Atlanta because they didn't want to hurt the attendance.

Bob Jones ultimately decided where the cameras were to be placed. One thing he said was that he wanted a camera in the middle of the fairway, if we could get it. He wanted to see the shots that were required, what a man had to do, what was the challenge that he was faced with, such as if he were on the fifteenth hole: How far down the fairway off the tee did he have to be before he could try to go over the water and go for the green with his second shot? There were a lot of decisions to be made. I remember Bob saying, "You can have all the cameras on the green that you want, but basically all a camera on the green shows you is that if a round object gets struck it will roll."

In 1956, we put the cameras in place, although in those days we did only the last three and a half holes. Bob wanted that camera at fifteen as discussed so the second shot could be shown from behind. But the only way we could do that was to have a mobile camera that could be latched onto a tractor and moved out onto the fairway after players had hit their drives at fifteen. Then we would line up the camera behind them, and after they had hit their second shots, we would have to quickly get that tractor out of the fairway so that the next group could hit. And that's the way fifteen was covered in the first year. We didn't have any balloons overhead in those days—we had to use a dadgum tractor.

—————

Former CBS-TV executive producer for golf **Frank Chirkinian** *spent nearly forty years directing Masters Tournament telecasts, beginning in 1958, giving him ample opportunity to interact with the likes of Jones and Roberts. The relationship between Augusta National and CBS-TV over the years has been a tenuous one, with CBS usually in the position of trying to produce the best telecast it can while walking on eggshells around club officials. This is one sporting event in which the network buying the rights for telecasting the event doesn't get to call all the production shots. In the days when Jones and Roberts both were still alive and running the tournament, they would offer comments and suggestions to CBS about how to improve or otherwise modify the telecast.*

Chirkinian often was the man in the middle of these debriefings, which ranged from the trivial to important considerations such as who comprised the broadcasting talent each year. It hasn't been an adversarial relationship between club and network, although CBS has long known that Augusta National could always choose to go with another network on a whim, and the Masters Tournament is the crown jewel of the network's annual golf coverage, if not its entire sports coverage. One aspect of this ongoing relationship is that together, Augusta National and CBS have forged golf coverage that has been clearly innovative and imitated.

During Masters week of his early years with CBS, Chirkinian spent a lot of time interacting with Jones and Roberts, giving him plenty of opportunities to get to know Jones up close and personal. It was a professional relationship, sure, but it was one that had to be built on mutual respect and trust:

I have never sat around and had drinks with him (Jones). We did chat on those rare occasions. He was insightful. One of the things that Bob passed on to me early on was about the television coverage. There were two things about the coverage that he pointed out to me which I found to be insightful, and I just kind of carried on with. The first was, he said, whatever you do, show a lot of golf. And that's what we did. We kind of developed that kind of coverage, even though there were several critics that did not like the idea. They called it the machine-gun technique: shot after shot after shot. After a while, I realized that this was kind of a synthetic drama that we were able to develop for those early rounds that were, of course, inconclusive. We knew we would not have a winner on Saturday, for instance, so we showed as much golf as we could, staying away from all of those profile things that the other networks were doing, stuff that was more of an outgrowth of the Olympics coverage from 1964. The other thing that he really impressed on me more than anything else is the fact that, "Don't talk about the money. The money really is superfluous." It does not mean anything. It is spent and gone. The memory of the championship, the token that is given to play in the championship, is what stays with you forever. Once the money is dissipated, that's it. The memory of the actual championship is the thing that lingers forever. That is always what you refer to, and you're referred to as a winner (not *champion*) of whatever it is that you've won. But he was really very much down on the financial aspect of golf. It was never the criteria as far as he was concerned.

I did my first golf telecast, the PGA Championship, in Philadelphia in 1958. Then in '60 I changed the scoring system for our golf coverage to a plus-or-minus system. Bob commended me for that, and he said that it certainly made the competition easier to recognize with this plus-or-minus system as opposed to extrapolating scores, because before we would put up a score of, say, Joe Smith, 256, and then you would have to figure out by yourself what that meant in terms of where that player stood against the rest of the field.

The man was probably the most hospitable, the most intelligent, and one of the most sensitive human beings I have ever known in my entire life. He impressed me tremendously. No question about it, he had an effect on how I did things in my career.

It's hard to say which was responsible for the other—was it CBS-TV's presence and production savvy that made the Masters into, arguably, the world's greatest televised golf event; or was it the beauty and allure of Augusta National and its Masters field of great champions that comprised a broadcasting coup that elevated CBS-TV to the forefront of golf coverage? It was probably some of both, helped along by the emergence in 1958 of handsome, broad-shouldered Arnold Palmer as a new Masters winner that men, women, and children all could adore.

One thing is certain, however: Augusta National is the most familiar golf venue to hundreds of millions of golf fans world-wide, and its beauty truly justifies its reputation, as former CBS golf honcho **Frank Chirkinian** *explains:*

I don't know if it was as much Bob as it was the golf course. I think it was the venue itself that perpetuated and developed the mystique, and continued the mystique, about the Masters. It's the only one of the four major championships that is played at the same site year after year. It's the sort of thing where a viewer could tune into any television broadcast of the Masters in mid-broadcast and know exactly what hole they're watching. There's a great sense of comfort and familiarity with the golf course. That's got an awful lot to do with how this thing grew. I am not standing up front trying to accept kudos or anything, but our industry had a lot to do with where Augusta is today.

I was a Bob Jones fan for a long time. I would look at slow-motion pictures of his swing and one day I sat (Tom) Weiskopf down and said, "I want you to see something." So Tommy and I watched this in slow motion and stopped Bob Jones's swing freeze-frame a number of times. What we saw was that his backswing was so long that he had to let go of the club with his left hand at the very top of his swing. To generate the torque to get back and deliver a strike, a blow, a forceful blow, to the golf ball because he was very long—and he was long with hickory shafts—is an amazing thing. How was he able to do it? My theory is that the reason he retired—and this is something that I have studied and thought about and, in fact, I queried Weiskopf about it, and in a way Tommy agreed with me—I think Bob Jones might have retired in '30 because he could not make the transition to steel (shafts). He could play that way where his swing would work with hickory, but it couldn't work with steel. Now think about that. He was way below parallel on his backswing, so much so that he let go of the club with his left hand. There was about a one-inch gap between his palm and the grip itself on the top of his swing. That is the way he generated enough torque with the hickory-shafted clubs to drive the ball as far as he did.

It's interesting to speculate what steel shafts would have done to Jones's swing; how he would have had to adjust. It would certainly have altered his swing, and I guess it was something that he did not seem to master, I don't know. It's an interesting theory and I have never espoused this theory publicly, but I always felt that there was something about the transition from hickory to steel that prompted him to retire and to decide, "This is not working and I'm not going to continue to do it."

—————

Atlanta native and crack amateur **Tommy Barnes,** *one of Jones's young cohorts, got to play in the Masters once. That one shot gave him a chance to make a nice contribution to the tournament and to see how it was run, even though he didn't come close to winning:*

I did get to play in the Masters once. That was in 1950 as a result of being first alternate for the U.S. Walker Cup team in 1949. I shot 304 and Jimmy Demaret won with 283, so I guess I didn't do too bad. I can't forget the first round of the tournament that year, which at the time was played a week earlier than they do now. It was thirty-nine degrees and the wind must have been blowing twenty miles an hour. But I didn't leave the tournament that week until I had some input into the tournament that was followed. I was with Clifford Roberts Tuesday night of that week in the dining room because he had motioned me over to sit with him. At one point he said to me, "Tom, we've got to do something about this damn slow play."

And I said, "What are you talking about, Mr. Roberts?"

"It's a crying shame we have to take four and a half hours to play this golf course with no rough."

"Mr. Roberts, you can't cut the time down but one way."

"Well, how in the world are you going to do that?"

And I said, "Play them in twosomes." They started playing twosomes soon after that. Shoot, playing twosomes, we went around there in under three hours.

---

*When **Tommy Jacobs** competed in the Masters Tournament for the first time, in 1952, he established a record that still stands as the youngest competitor ever to qualify for the event. Jacobs was seventeen at the time and somewhat in awe of playing in such a special tournament that featured an incomparable field of golfers that represented historical significance as well as excellence. By then, Jones's health was failing and opportunities to see him or talk to him were becoming fewer and more precious with each passing year:*

I spent more time that week in 1952 around Cliff Roberts than I did around Jones. Jones would get out in his cart—at times they were together, but mostly separate. I remember meeting him and being in awe, but I didn't really get to know him. His health was starting to fail him at this time. I had read an awful lot about Jones. Hogan and Hagen also were idols of mine; Horton Smith, too. Jones's book *Golf Is My Game* remains one of my most cherished golf books I ever bought.

Augusta National was Jones's baby, and at that time it was his life represented by his involvement in creating one of the greatest golf courses and tournaments. That's why they tweak it practically every year, although I think they went too far recently when they tried to curtail it for the long hitters. The more they lengthen it and toughen it, as they recently did in growing out the rough more, the more they play into the hands of the long hitters like Tiger Woods. What always made Augusta so great was that there were

Jones draws a crowd teeing off at Augusta during a practice round before the 1937 Masters. (AP/Wide World Photos)

always several people who could win it coming down to the wire, and I guarantee you if Jones were still alive today, he would not allow for these recent changes. I think all Jones would have done perhaps is move some of the tees back and soften up the fairways a little bit. I mean, even when Tiger's hitting a short iron into the par-fives for his second shots, the other guys are at least hitting irons themselves, too, so what's the problem with the way it was?

Although the Masters hadn't yet emerged as the unparalleled television event it is today, in 1952 it was already a very big deal for the players. But it's a bigger deal all-around now because the media has grown so much. I don't know how many credentials they used to pass out in those days, but if they passed out a hundred then, they probably pass out twelve hundred now.

Back when I first played in the Masters, I was staying in a small trailer adjacent to the clubhouse, and my roommate in the trailer was Johnny Dawson. Being around there for the first time, I was just awestruck. You're floating on cloud nine. It was either on a Monday or Tuesday when I was playing a practice round with Johnny Dawson—and was already just in awe—when I met Jones out on the golf course. We were on one of the tees and he just drove up. He and Johnny were already good friends. Keep in mind that Jones had a certain affinity for amateurs, and Johnny was one of the top amateurs in the country then. I wasn't particularly nervous in meeting him, but I got nervous when it came time for the first round of the tournament. My first round was 77 and I ended up averaging 79 for the four rounds—they didn't have a cut in those days.

Like most other Masters winners before him and since, **Doug Ford** *had to "learn" how to win at Augusta National, a feat that usually involves two things: becoming familiar with the course's idiosyncrasies and dealing with the back-nine pressure on a Masters Sunday:*

I remember losing it the year before, when I shot a 42 on the back side after being tied for the lead teeing off at the tenth. Then in '57 I was in the same position and shot 32 on the back nine to go past (Sam) Snead. The back nine there either makes you or breaks you. Experience is what counts. You can't fight that back nine (which includes Amen Corner comprised of holes eleven through thirteen), you have to be able to wait and take your chances at the right holes. You can't try to birdie everything all at once.

If you analyze Augusta National and how it was laid out and set up, I would have to say that it indicates what a great putter Jones was. He must have been a good driver, but driving isn't the thing you have to do best there. It's your iron play and the putting that are the keys. Those greens are unreal—you can't believe how tough they are. The undulations in the greens, as they were originally, were tough enough, but now that they've put bent-grass in the greens, they're unbelievably fast. The original course was much shorter, as was the case with the eleventh hole. It wasn't the hard hole it is now.

I think what he was doing, in his thinking in helping to design the course, was making a good golf course for membership play more so than for championship play. But it evolved because they had enough land with which to lengthen the course, and now with the rough grown up it's gotten really big. I don't think Jones liked rough. He left himself plenty of room for the landing areas on the drive. Driving wasn't the key then that it is now, and I think they've put something like four hundred or five hundred yards on it since the year that I won (1957). You can feel your way around when not to go for it and when to go for it.

I played a lot of games with Snead there. I can remember on the second hole there, one day, where he took his driver and poured it over the hill and then knocked it onto the green. The next day while going to the second tee, I turned to (Bob) Goalby and said, "I'm going to hit a three-wood off the tee here. Ask me why, because Snead has rabbit ears, you know." I then said, a bit louder, "I wouldn't take a chance here, because if you go a little left, you're talking six or seven. I'll just lay back and then try going at the green with my third shot." I get up there and hit my three-wood, and Goalby steps up and hits his three-wood, and then Snead gets up there, goes with his three-wood, and he duck-hooks it into the trees from where he made something like an eight. That was pretty funny. You've got to really think and play the right shot off the tee at Augusta.

In reminiscing about his Masters Tournament triumph in 1957, **Doug Ford** *remembers the tournament as being much lower-keyed than the worldwide coronation it has turned into over the last couple of decades:*

I don't remember Jones in that ceremony. I have a picture of (Jackie) Burke (who had won the Masters the previous year) putting the green jacket on me and that's about all that I remember about that. At that time, the green coat ceremony wasn't as big an event as it is now. It has been blown all out of proportion by the media.

Jones talked mostly to guys like Snead, who had played golf with him. I was too much in awe of him—he was "Mr. Jones" to me. Some of these kids nowadays don't know Jones from Joe Blow.

Winning the Masters didn't really change my life that much. The tournament I won that really changed my life was the PGA Championship that I had won in 1955. The PGA Championship in those days gave you a lifetime exemption from having to qualify for the PGA Tour. That's a big edge. In those days, winning the Masters, as far as I can remember, didn't give you any exemptions into any tournaments, except theirs. My having won the Masters means a lot more to me today than it did forty years ago.

Ford played in enough Masters to get a good feel for how Jones and Roberts joined forces in making Augusta National and the Masters true phenomenons:

It was a combination of both. Roberts took a lot of his leads from Jones. I know that. He was the front man. I don't think Jones wanted to be considered a force of any kind; he was just an adviser-like. He was on top of everything until he couldn't do it anymore. I never got much of a chance to talk with Jones, except, "Hello" and "How are you feeling."

Former CBS-TV golf announcer **John Derr** *was there working at Augusta during Masters week in the early days of television coverage, and he recalls some of the foibles that went into making each telecast a success—thanks, in part, to Jones:*

For the first dozen or more years of CBS television coverage of the Masters, beginning in 1956, one of my assignments was to dash up from the fifteenth green location to the Butler Cabin alongside the clubhouse. There I would introduce Jones and Mr. Roberts for the ceremony honoring the winner, putting on the green jacket and all.

If I ran fast enough I could sit with Jones as we watched the closing holes on a monitor. Often he would have meaningful comments about the play and players.

It was during this interval at the 1965 tournament when Jack Nicklaus was spread-eagling the field that Jones turned from the monitor and made his oft-quoted evaluation—perhaps the greatest praise ever accorded Jack's game—"Nicklaus is playing a game with which I am not familiar."

Jones was not speaking for immortality. He was voicing an opinion from his own background of excellence.

Jones was a man of unusual skills and unlimited vision. In the fall of 1955 we were touring the Augusta National course in a station wagon, surveying where cameras should be located for the television coverage the next April.

"We may as well determine locations on all eighteen holes," Jones told the CBS-TV crew. "They are not doing it yet, but one of these days television will cover all eighteen holes."

This was at a time when cameras covered only the last three or four holes. No one dared think of covering all eighteen, the logistics being so primitive. But Jones foresaw that day.

He was more than just a golfer. That may have been one of his lesser traits; he worked at it less than some others. He was an engineer, a lawyer, an author, and an administrator. He was a traditionalist but at the same time an innovator.

I was fortunate to have had him as a friend, encouraging me to keep looking ahead, trying to improve my profession, saying uphill was easier, if the goal was in view. He helped me understand competitive golf and made my reporting more factual, and hopefully more interesting. His suggestions were always to the point, never cruel, always helpful.

Jones never tried to improve my playing—that was too much of a challenge, even for Jones. But with his help I became a better reporter and broadcaster of his sport.

Born on Saint Patrick's Day in 1902, Jones died at the age of sixty-nine, one week before Christmas in 1971.

We knew the end was near, blessedly so, for he had suffered valiantly those final months. When I got the call that Jones had died, I immediately went to my home club and requested the membership flag be lowered to half-staff.

"What member died?" the attendant asked.

Sadly I informed him it was the great Bob Jones. That man in Atlanta should be considered a member—and honored member, not an honorary member—at this and every other club where golf is played. So it was, signaling universal sorrow, the flag flew in mourning until his funeral.[8]

―――

Dozens of men have won the Masters Tournament over the years, but none of them under as much a shroud of controversy as **Bob Goalby,** *who won the 1968 Masters when Roberto DeVicenzo inadvertently signed an incorrect scorecard that* *added a stroke to his final score. That one stroke came at the seventeenth hole on Sunday, where playing partner Tommy Aaron marked down a four on DeVicenzo's scorecard instead of the birdie three that he had actually made. Once DeVicenzo signed the incorrect scorecard without changing his score at the seventeenth, the Rules of Golf made Goalby the winner by one shot over the now-runner-up DeVicenzo. Goalby, a fine golfer in his own right, has long since had an asterisk beside his name, in a figurative sense and certainly not by his choice, although he keeps close at hand a letter that Jones sent to him making it clear that Goalby deserved every bit the green jacket that he won:*

He was an elegant writer and speaker, you know, he was very good. He was well rounded and well read. This is a letter I got after I won the Masters.

Dear Bob,

The privilege of welcoming a new Masters champion to a green coat is something that I have always reserved to myself. I was especially disappointed this year that a virus attack caused it to be impossible for me to make the presentation to you. I am sending you my warm congratulations on my first day back in circulation. Your golf in Augusta was superb in every way. I saw a good bit of it on the television monitor in my bedroom. [Goalby: He was at the tournament, but in his cottage.] I was particularly thrilled by those three great putts you holed at thirteen, fourteen, and fifteen of the last round and by your exquisite second shot to the fifteenth, which was the finest shot I have ever seen played on that hole.

The scorecard mix-up was a tragedy for Roberto, but it was also one of equal proportions for you. I thought you both handled the situation in the most sportsmanlike and exemplary manner. I know you would have much preferred to go to a playoff, but I ask you always to remember that you won the tournament under the Rules of Golf and by a superlative play. Indeed, I think overall, it was the most beautifully contested tournament I have ever seen. We, at Augusta, will always be proud of you as a Masters champion. I hope that this will prove to be only the beginning of a wonderful year for you. I shall look forward to seeing you next spring.

With warmest regards.

Most sincerely,
Bob Jones

It's a beautiful letter. That is why I have it framed. I thought it was beautiful coming from him because of his stature in golf.

Jones wasn't involved much with what happened until the end. I was two groups behind Roberto, and he was playing with Tommy Aaron. Roberto made a birdie at seventeen, but Aaron ended up putting a four down on the card. But you've got to keep in mind that the player himself has the sole responsibility for signing his own card and seeing that it is correct. We all have that responsibility and it almost has to be that way because I don't want anyone else turning my card in unless I see it. It's unfortunate that Aaron put that four down, but Roberto didn't check his card, evidently. Some guys do that, and I think he might have been mad because he had just made a (bogey) five at eighteen. He might have figured that he lost it because I was one ahead at that time. But I three-putted seventeen and that made us tied. I then made a four at eighteen, making a four-footer for what I thought was a tie, and then when I got to the scorer's table, everybody was pretty much hush-hush. I was just pretty pleased that I had made the four-footer to tie, right? Everybody was kind of subdued. No one was saying anything like "Nice putt, Bob," when usually there would be at least somebody excited.

There wasn't too much going on and I didn't know what was going on, but I didn't think too much of it because I went and got my card all taken care of. Then when I was walking away, Cary Middlecoff, who was working for CBS then, was right there by the edge of the green and he said to me, "Bob, you won this tournament," and I said, "What!?" He said, "There's a problem with DeVicenzo's scorecard and he's out. You've won." And that was the first time that I sensed there was any problem. Doc, who had won twice there as a player, was a little more attuned to what had happened with the rule. I guess they hem-and-hawed around for a little while, and you've got to remember that I had been two holes behind Roberto. After he had signed his card, they had gone to Jones, and when Middlecoff saw me, I think, is when they had just gotten word back from Jones, saying, "Boys, as you know, we play by the rules here, and the rules here say that it's over." That was about all I know about it.

When I was a kid, all I ever seemed to read about was Bobby Jones. I started caddying in 1938, and he was still a big name around then. His name was on clubs and Spalding was a big clubmaker at that time. They had all of the business—all the balls and everything. You know how much a top of the line golf ball cost in 1929? Seventy-five cents. That's why very few people played the game then, even though the clubs weren't really all that expensive by comparison. I remember when I started caddying in the late thirties and early forties, if you lost a ball it was like the world came to an end. You didn't get a tip. But then it's easy to see why, at seventy-five cents a ball. That was a lot, especially back then. They kept golf balls in that price range until right after the war, when they went to eighty-five cents.

Getting back to the letter I got from Mr. Jones, it told me that he didn't talk about himself very much. He never did talk about what he had done. He just talked about the great game of golf, like he did when he spoke when we were playing the 1963 Ryder Cup Matches at East Lake, where he grew up and played the game for the first time. He was very eloquent when he spoke, not necessarily with monstrous words but with words you seldom heard spoken by the average golfer. He was well cultivated and he traveled a lot when he was young, and I guess his parents taught him well. I remember Jones being around for the Ryder Cup Matches in 1963, and he came and gave a talk at the main dinner with both Ryder Cup teams there, all the players with their wives and the Ryder Cup officials as well. He gave a nice speech, very elegant.

Goalby had actually met Jones five years earlier, when Jones turned out to meet the U.S. Ryder Cup team prior to the 1963 Matches, which were held at Jones's home golf course, East Lake Country Club in Atlanta. Goalby got another introduction to Jones while preparing for one of the Masters Tournaments in the sixties, courtesy of practice-round playing partner Sam Snead, who had the playful audacity to ask Jones if it was okay

*to use one of the ponds at Augusta National for a little bit of
fishing:*

I didn't know him before that (the 1963 Ryder Cup). I met
him at the Masters in the sixties when I was playing there. I
played a lot of practice rounds with Sam (Snead), almost
every year at least one of the practice rounds with him, and
this went on for thirty years. One time we were going to
twelve and crossing the bridge, when Jones drove up in his
cart, with Cliff Roberts. They said, "Hello, Sam, how are you
doing?" and this and that, and Jones talked to all four of us
playing the practice round. Being that we were at the bridge,
Sam said to him, "Hey, Bob, do you mind if I wet my line?"
There were fish in the pond that you could see when you
went around the par-three. Jones stood there a while and
finally he said, "All right, Sam, it would be all right, but
don't keep them when you catch them. Throw them back
in." A few years later, one of the young pros and his family,
and I don't want to tell you who it was so as not to embar-
rass him, pulled his station wagon up to the dam and had
something like a picnic with his kids. They were all fishing
in the lake and that was after Cliff (Roberts) was gone (dead,
by a self-inflicted gunshot wound). If Jones and Cliff had
been there, he probably wouldn't have gotten to play. And
you think, jeez, Snead had to beg just to wet his line down
there, let alone have a picnic on the dam.

Another time I was down there at Augusta National
early, before the start of another Masters, and was getting a
haircut from the barber who had been there like forty years.
We were looking out the window and saw some beer bottles
out on the table. I think it was like a Monday morning. And
he says to me, "You see that out there? That never would

have happened had Cliff and Bob been here. There would not have been one thing out of place out there." That's just another of the little things that come to mind when I think about Jones.

There's another good story that Freddie Haas (also a golfer) told me. He was kind of an inventor, always inventing new things to try out. One thing he invented was a gooseneck driver before they made them. This was like forty or fifty years ago. Jones was a big man with Spalding at that time, and Haas told Jones about his gooseneck club. He wanted to show it to him and asked if he could come show it and Jones said, "Sure, why don't you come over to my office." So Freddie drove over to Atlanta from New Orleans with this new club that he was sure was going to revolutionize the game and make it easier for the average player and therefore more people could enjoy the game. That was Freddie's theory. He's the one who told me the story. Freddie said that after he told Jones all this, not that it would really help the superstars, and Jones said, "Freddie, I'm not interested in making this game easier for just anybody. This game is for a select few." Now whether or not that is actually true, I don't know, but it is a pretty good story.

—⁂—

Nearly four decades of directing CBS-TV's telecasts of the Masters gave **Frank Chirkinian** *ample opportunity to study Augusta National, the course and the club, and in the process to learn more about the personalities of cofounders Bobby Jones and Clifford Roberts:*

There were two different attitudes. One was aesthetic and

one was pragmatic. Roberts was the pragmatist. But Bob Jones did say to me one time that a golf course is like a living creature, that it must be in a constant state of change to survive. He was a strong advocate of making changes. Very much so. I can't remember a year in my thirty-eight years that I televised that tournament where there wasn't some change made somewhere, some very subtle things sometimes that nobody notices. He was an advocate of that.

Roberts was a businessman, and he had a different attitude toward these things than Bob Jones did. Bob Jones was not interested in business (of golf). His interest, of course, was golf and nothing but golf. The only identification with Bob Jones is with golf, certainly not with Bob Jones the legal mind, the lawyer; or Bob Jones whatever else, say, the businessman. Nobody ever referred to Bob Jones in those terms. That was the role that Roberts played. In fact, it was Roberts who insisted on calling it the Masters. Bob Jones had conjured up the idea of calling it the Masters Invitational. Roberts never liked the invitational aspect of it and just wanted to call it the Masters. Which he (Roberts) did prevail and eventually Jones did concede that it was a better title for the tournament. Together, they came up with something pretty special.

4

ROLE MODEL

Bobby Jones wasn't a saint. He drank, he smoked, and he uttered the occasional profanity. But as the greatest golf champion of the first half of the twentieth century, Jones was a model of sportsmanship who cared as much about promoting the game as mastering it.

Even without television in his day, he was a media sensation, dominating sports headlines and later becoming a pioneer in the making of instructional videos. Citizens could catch glimpses of Jones in action by going out to the local picture show and viewing newsreels that might include something as revelatory as a single swing, more often than not posed just for the camera. Even then, relatively few people ever got to see much of Jones's classic full, flowing swing, so young golfers looking for a swing model to emulate were best off learning the game by caddying for good golfers at their local club and emulating the swings of those that looked useful.

What people couldn't see of Jones's swing they could read about. He wrote three books on golf, starting with *Down the Fairway* when he was just twenty-five years old. As humble and occasionally self-effacing as he was forthcoming and insightful, Jones dissected the game, the swing, and course

Here Jones blasts from a bunker in an Optimists Golf Tournament held sometime after he had retired from competitive golf. (AP/Wide World Photos)

strategy in ways that would serve as primers for how to play the game as well as enjoy it. One of many testaments to Jones's enduring status as a role model is the existence of "Down the Fairway with Bobby Jones," a permanent exhibition on golf in Georgia that was opened at the Atlanta History Center.

———

Count **Herbert Warren Wind** *among the many sports scribes who over the years have painted a picture of Jones that was almost bigger than life:*

(Jones) was the model American athlete come to life. Everybody adored him—not just dyed-in-the-wool golfers, but people who had never struck a golf ball or had the least desire to. They admired the ingrained modesty, the humor, the generosity of spirit that were evident in Jones's remarks and deportment. They liked the way he looked, this handsome, clean-cut young man, whose eyes gleamed with both a frank boyishness and a perceptiveness far beyond his years.[1]

———

Author and hero-worshipper **Paul Gallico** *touched on Jones in his book* Farewell to Sport:

I am, by nature, a hero-worshipper, as, I guess, most of us are, but in all the years of contact with the famous ones of sport I have found only one that would stand up in every way as a gentleman as well as a celebrity, a fine, decent, human being as well as a newsprint personage, and who never once, since I have known him, has let me down in my estimate of him.

111

That one is Robert Tyre Jones Jr., the golf-player from Atlanta, Georgia. And Jones in his day was considered the champion of champions.[2]

---

*Of all the contemporary golf figures that could, in any way, be compared to Jones, **Ben Crenshaw** might come the closest; if not in terms of major championships won, at least in other factors such as physique, character, golfing excellence as a teenager, and deep appreciation for the traditions of the game. Crenshaw is quite likely the most historically astute professional golfer of his generation, and the fact that his two major titles have both come at the Masters and Augusta solidify his place in golf history as well as his ties to the late, great Jones. Writing in the book* American Golfer, *this is some of what Crenshaw had to say about Jones:*

Robert Tyre Jones, Jr. will forever be in a class by himself to my way of thinking. And I am not alone, by any means. For from this man we learn not only how we may improve our golf games and act like gentlemen, but also how to cope with life, however good or bad it may be. As Herbert Warren Wind has said, "As a young man he was able to stand up to just about the best that life can offer, and later he stood up with equal grace to just about the worst." Millions of words have been written about Bob Jones, but this quote sums it up. We can never quite describe the man he was; we can only try to learn from his example what golf and life are all about.[3]

Freddie Haas is one of the remaining few who's old enough to have played against Jones when Jones was still a serious competitor. Haas was there to see the creation of Augusta National and the inception of a tournament that came to be known as the Masters. Haas, being more than ten years younger than Jones, really wasn't a peer of Jones's, but he did grow up in the golf world at a time when Jones was still generating headlines as a player and capturing young golfers' fancies with a free-flowing swing as efficient as it was powerful.

Haas is a national treasure when it comes to golf in America, a former touring pro who matched shots with Jones, rubbed elbows with the likes of Nelson and Hogan, mentored players in the Palmer and Nicklaus generations, and witnessed the emergence of golfers the likes of Trevino, Watson, Strange, and Woods. Haas has seen it all and been an active part of much of it. In recalling Jones and what Jones meant to golf, Haas takes us down an old dusty trail to the setting of what life was like for young golfers of his generation, growing up in the shadow of Jones:

When I was a young amateur, we would all try to emulate Bobby Jones because we thought he was marvelous. This was from 1924 until 1928. After that, when he won the Grand Slam (in 1930), well, then we knew he really was the one and we became much more enthralled with his great victories.

In 1928 I played in a tournament at Augusta, Georgia—we were living in the Carolinas at that time; I was twelve years old—I shot 40 on the front nine and forgot what I shot on the back nine, which really doesn't matter because Bobby Jones, also playing in the tournament, won it by something like twelve strokes over Horton Smith. This was played at

Augusta Country Club and a course at Forest Hills, and it was way before the Masters and Augusta National had come into existence.

The next time I ran across Bobby Jones was when I saw his teachings at the picture shows. He made a series of instructional films, and, of course, I was quite interested in those. I was still in high school. I was extremely interested in going to college at that time, and the only way I could go was by getting a scholarship, which I got from the University of Arkansas, and the only scholarships they gave were to the high school golf winners. By then, we were living in a little cotton town in Arkansas by the name of Dermott, which is about seventy miles south of Pine Bluff. That being the case with golf scholarships and being able to afford to go to college, my family was very interested in getting me to play golf—except that we didn't have a golf course in Dermott. We had to ride about forty miles to Eudora to play golf, and this was over gravel roads. Invariably, we would have a flat tire or whatever, so it was quite a chore to get out and play golf.

I was fortunate to play golf once a week. They had sand greens and there were cows out there, and we had a bit of a problem with the cows. Every now and then we would be able to go to Monticello, where they had a golf course, a nine-hole course—all of these courses in those days, at least the ones I was able to get to, were nine holes. Finally, Dad and I decided we had to build a golf course in Dermott. We had enough land right on the other side of the railroad tracks, so we built a course with five greens and made enough tees so as to make it an eighteen-hole course. That's why I was able to play golf a lot more frequently there. This was in 1931.

We saw the picture shows in Dermott. It cost us all of a

dime or quarter to see them, but nobody had any money at that time. It was quite a chore to get that money, but we thought it was important enough to do it so we could go see the shows. We saw the instructional films featuring Jones, and they were very good. We sure latched on to them. Some of what we saw in these instructional films was very good and some of it was very bad, and this was something I cleared with Bobby Jones about twenty years later. The thing that was good for me is that I was able to play every day, and I was able to then win the Arkansas state high school championship two years in a row.

I was given a scholarship to the University of Arkansas and I was planning on going there, until Dad turned pro at the golf course, and with the cotton business going down, he had to make a few bucks. He was called to Bastrop, Louisiana, to take over the clubhouse at the Monroe Country Club, which had a nine-hole course. So we went down there—sometime in June, after my senior year in high school. My uncle, who was a state senator in Louisiana, said to me, "Freddie, why don't you come down and play in the Louisiana state championship in Baton Rouge." And I said, "Sure, I'd love to do it." This was right after we had moved to Bastrop. They had a Calcutta there and someone bought me for six dollars.

A guy by the name of Edwin McClure was the defending champion, and he was expected to win again. He sold for several thousand dollars. But I went on and qualified for the championship flight and won three matches, and all of a sudden I'm in the semifinals playing Edwin McClure. Of course, I'm expected to get beat, but I didn't do that. I beat him, and so now I'm in the finals in the Louisiana state championship. The other fellow who got to the finals, also by quite a surprise, was a guy by the name of Bobby Anderson, a freshman at LSU. Bobby could hit the ball good, but had had practically no experience playing in tournaments. I was five down with five to go, and just about that time who comes up, but my uncle, accompanied by Huey Long. I won the fourteenth and fifteenth holes and now we're playing the sixteenth hole, and I hit my second shot right in front of the green and it looks like I might have a chance to win that. But there was an unusual slope. I hit my third shot over the green and wound up losing the hole and the match. When we got through, Huey Long came up to me and said, "Hey, your uncle here says that you can get me the best golf team in America and we want you to play on it and get some other guys here and put LSU on the map in terms of golf." And I said, "That's very nice, but I'm going to the University of Arkansas on a golf scholarship." And he says, "Nah, the heck you are. I want you to come to LSU."

The next day I met Huey Long outside the stadium at LSU and we were talking and he said, "Now, I want you to go out and get some guys. You know who can play and who can't play, and it looks like you can play." Now, I've forgotten whether he was senator or governor at that time. I said, "One thing that's going to be a problem here is, Where in the world are we going to play? You don't have anything here at the school." He said, "We'll worry about that." I then looked around and pointed to a place across the street and said, "You see those cows over there? There's a nice place over there. It would be close to the school and everybody can play. We can build a course there."

"Oh, no, son," he said, "I can't afford to move those cows. Every farmer in the state would revolt against me if I did anything to displace cows."

I said, "Well, we've got to find a place to play."

And he said, "I'll make arrangements for you to play the Westdale Golf Club."

I said, "How are we going to get out there to play?"

And he said, "We'll figure out a way."

It must have been thirty-five miles out there. Anyway, he got the governor-elect, and the governor-elect got us an old truck and would get us a tank of gas, and every night the football players would siphon the gas out of our truck. We had a heckuva time playing, but somehow we were able to manage.

At the time I knew guys like Horton Smith, Harry Cooper, Jimmy Thompson, and Lawson Little, who were going around the country giving exhibitions. They were some of the top players of that day (Smith won the first Masters in 1934, when the event was called, simply, the Annual Invitational). I got in touch with Horton Smith, whom I had met in 1928 when he won the tournament in Hot Springs. I asked him to come down and open up the Westdale Country Club, after I had sold the university on the idea of buying the golf course. We had a tough time raising $25,000 to buy the course, but we finally did it, and I think it's because the football team went to the Sugar Bowl around that time. Those four guys came down and played an exhibition with our golf team, and that's how we opened that golf course. I had gotten some good players, such as Paul Leslie, whom I had played in the Western Junior. Another guy was Wright Adams, from Arkansas. We had fairly good success. The big tournaments were played up North, but I was fortunate to win the NCAAs in 1937 and Paul was the runner-up to me. Meanwhile, Paul had won the Western Amateur.

Dad eventually took the job as head pro at Colonial Country Club in New Orleans the same year they had the Southern Amateur Championships at the New Orleans Country Club. I won that tournament. I was a sophomore at LSU. That fall, Bobby Jones came to New Orleans to play an exhibition at the Metairie Country Club. The people there invited me to play with Bobby Jones. I was so honored to get the chance to play with him. When we got through playing, Bobby came up to me and says, "Fred, you've got a chance of playing really well, and I'm looking for some up-and-coming amateurs to play in my tournament that I'm going to have next year at Augusta National Golf Club and we're going to call it the Masters. I'd like to invite you to play with Charlie Yates and a couple of other young amateurs. Would you like to play?" And I said, "Yes, sir." So I played in the first Masters and from that time on I was able to meet with Bobby and get to know him.

I had a couple of nice visits with him. One of the most pleasant experiences I had meeting with him was sitting next to him for the dinner for the Walker Cup players before we went overseas to play the English players in 1938. We were able to renew acquaintances and it was very nice. I played in quite a few of the Masters early on. One year I got in because of my Walker Cup status; another year I got voted in by the past winners of the Masters; and another time I got in because I had finished in the top twenty-four the year before. In the early fifties I got in once because I had played on a Ryder Cup team. So I got into the Masters thanks to a wide variety of invitational criteria.

*Writer **Herbert Warren Wind** describes Jones as a golfer who was tougher on himself than on his competition, if you can believe that, considering how dominating he was at times in winning tournaments:*

Bobby did learn more about putting his shots together as he toured the country playing Red Cross exhibitions during the war, but it took him a good while longer to learn how to control his temper. Young Jones knew he was a crackerjack golfer, just as every pretty girl knows she is a pretty girl, but Bobby was not a prima donna in the sense that he demanded special attention and kid-glove handling. On the contrary, he was an exemplary sportsman in all his dealings with other people, so much so, as he grew older, that more than one of his rivals remarked that a chief reason why Bobby never won a championship was that he went out of his way too much to comfort and cheer his opponents when they hit a bad streak. But with himself Bobby was rough. The target of Jones's tantrums was always Bobby Jones, the dope who was continually making some inexcusable error, missing some silly shot through carelessness and lack of concentration.[4]

―――――

Speaking about the temper, here's some light that Jones shed on the subject:

It wasn't an easy matter . . . It's sort of hard to explain, unless you play golf yourself, and have a temper. You see, I never lost my temper with an opponent. I was angry only with myself. It always seemed, and it seems today, such an utterly useless and idiotic thing to stand up to a perfectly simple shot, one that I know I can make a hundred times running without a miss—and then mess up the blamed thing, the one time I want to make it! And it's gone forever—an irrevocable crime, that stroke . . . I think it was Stevenson who said that bad men and fools eventually got what was coming to them, but the fools first. And when you feel so extremely a fool, and a bad golfer to boot, what the deuce can you do, except throw the club away? . . . Well, well—Chick Evans, writing years later, said I had conquered my temper not wisely but too well; that a flare now and then would help me. I liked that of Chick.[5]

Perhaps the most significant key in the golf swing involves the wrists. One of the great mysteries in golf has long been the content of Ben Hogan's so-called "Secret," a concept that a number of swing experts have hypothesized as relating to the cocking of the wrists during the backswing. Hogan's key word in this regard was pronation. *Basically, the idea is, during the takeaway, to independently turn the wrists as far to the right (for a right-hander) and to keep the wrists so cocked through the backswing and down through to impact with the ball. Such a move supposedly adds clubhead speed and therefore increases power. Jones, long before Hogan, addressed this concept in his book* Bobby Jones on Golf:

An ample cocking of the wrists, and the retention of the greater part of this angle for use in the hitting area is not only important for good timing and increasing the speed of the club head: it is absolutely necessary in order to enable the player to

Jones pictured in 1942 in his Atlanta law office right after being commissioned a captain in the U.S. Army/Air Corps. He was set to report for active duty right after completing that year's National Hale America Tournament, a one-time substitute for the U.S. Open, in Chicago. (AP/Wide World Photos)

strike downward and so produce backspin. When the angle between the left arm and the shaft of the club becomes open too early in the downstroke, the club head at this point will be too low and the subsequent arc will be too flat.[6]

—⚬—

Any golfer who has ever received golf instruction from a better-skilled person has probably been exposed to various theories about weight shift during the swing. Here, Jones "weighs in" with his own thoughts on the touchy subject:

It is my definite opinion that there need be no shifting of weight from left foot to right during the backstroke. I have

121

examined numbers of photographs of the very best players, and I have been able to find no case in which such a shifting was perceptible; but there should occur during the hitting stroke a pronounced shift from right to left—a shift that does not follow the club, or pass smoothly along coincident with its progress, but is executed quickly, and leads the arms and club all the way through.[7]

Harvey Penick sheds some more light on the particulars of Jones's golf game:

Bobby Jones used the overlapping grip with the tip of his right forefinger not touching the handle at all. But the back of the first joint of his forefinger pressed against the handle. Victor East of Spalding built special grips with flat places for the back of Jones's right forefinger, which would be illegal today.[8]

*In getting to know Jones as an established touring pro, no longer an awestruck teenage golfer, **Freddie Haas** saw his confidence increase around Jones, and over the years he found himself discussing aspects of the golf swing. Haas remembered those old newsreels he had viewed in Dermott, Arkansas, as an aspiring high school golfer, and eventually his conversations with Jones worked their way around to the golf swing:*

The thing I remember vividly about Bobby Jones is that he had a hook when he wasn't swinging as well as he would have liked to, but he was able to do something that I don't know anyone else could do. He could hit a high hook, and the ball, instead of coming back too far, Bobby had a spin on the ball that it would sort of drift to the right a bit at the end. So he was able to stop the ball with those shots in a way that other people just couldn't seem to do.

Evidently, he could manage the ball much better than anyone else. That's one of the reasons I thought he was one of the great players. Plus the fact he could really, with the draw that he was able to put on the ball, outdrive a lot of people. One time he was playing with Horton Smith at that (1928) tournament in Augusta, and Bobby was outdriving him by fifty to seventy-five yards. Horton was playing a little left to right, and Bobby was hitting those high hooks and his ball would roll considerably longer than Horton's, and that's why he was able to win that tournament by what I think was twelve strokes over Horton. He just played beautifully; it was a great pleasure to watch him, and I saw every one of his shots after I got through playing myself.

Anyway, in getting back to when I was now playing the Masters in its early years, the next thing I know is that I'm out there one day practicing for the Masters at about six o'clock. I'm about through over on one side of the practice range, and about thirty-five yards away I see a fellow come out there with a bag of balls and a caddie to retrieve the balls. I wasn't paying too much attention to him and went on with what I was doing. After a while I turned around to look again and realized, Doggone, that's Bobby Jones over there! So I kind of moseyed over there to within about ten or twenty yards of him, and just sat down to watch him play. This is where I got the understanding that I had watched some of his fundamentals on film. I had been trying to copy them and I couldn't do it. It had always been a frustrating experience for me. This time, Bobby got to a point, while he

123

was practicing there, that he could not control his hook. He was standing farther and farther to the right to bring it in. He was hooking it while hitting the ball very low, and you could tell that it was a devastating result for such a beautiful swing.

I now understand, in looking back, that he was going about this all wrong because he was trying to play the hook, and he kept standing to the right and it got worse and worse and worse. He never played after that. He just could not get over the hook.

Not long after that, he got sick. I continued to play in his tournament, and then I got so that I had to do something with my swing and change the flight of the ball. So I said to myself, Something is happening here. I can't play like he played. He tilted his chest to the right and looked at the ball, and he got behind the ball beautifully and that's why he could hit that controlled hook. When I tried to do that, the ball was moving on me! But the ball wasn't really moving, so what the heck was going on? I realized then that it was my eyes that were causing the problem. I got to thinking, *For heaven's sake, there must be something wrong because surely Bobby didn't play that way.* So I called him up, and Bobby was in braces at that time. He had had an operation and was able to move around some. I called him up and he said to come over, "We'll talk this afternoon, if you want to." So I hopped a plane and went there to see him.

I got over there and said to him, "Bobby, you are the greatest golfer in the world, but somehow or other, when I saw you practicing out there, you were doing something that must have been frustrating to you. You couldn't control that hook," and he said, "That's right." I said, "Well, it looked to me like you started playing for it instead of trying to do the reverse. You kept trying to improve on something that wasn't working." And he said, "Exactly." So I said to him, "Tell me something now. I've been trying to follow your instructions, and I've got my chest pointed back and am trying to stay behind the ball. But the ball is moving on me! Now, I know the ball isn't really moving on me, but it's very distracting to me. Here's the conclusion that I've reached. I set up behind the ball and I cock my head to the right, I can still see the ball with my left eye and my right eye, but when I get up to the top of my backswing, I can no longer see the ball with my right eye. Based on what the eye doctors have told me, what I think is happening, when I'm setting up to the ball, I'm still looking at it with my right eye, but when I get up to the top of my swing, I can only see it with my left eye, and therefore my view of the ball is shifting from my right eye to my left. Then when I come through on my downswing, I'm picking the ball back up with my right eye, and that's what produces the effect of the ball 'moving' for me. If you point at an object and look at it, first close one eye and then the other, the darn thing moves two or three inches on you. That's what's happening to me with the golf ball." And he said, "Yeahhh?" And I said, "Well, Bobby, I'm only here to ask you a question. Are you left-handed? Do you write left-handed?"

"It's strange that you would ask," he said, "because I am left-handed. I'm left-everything."

"Then why are you playing golf right-handed?"

"That's another strange thing that you ask me. I couldn't get adequate clubs when I was young to play left-handed, so I decided early on that I was going to play golf right-handed."

"That seems like it was the right thing for you to do because with your being left-handed, your left eye never leaves the ball during your backswing."

"That's right, I don't have trouble with the ball moving. You know, I can remember that I wrote something one time about the dominant-eye theory, and I might have made some comment about that, but I can't remember what I said."

"Bobby, I want to thank you for telling me that because let me tell you what I have done. I had to play, instead of with my chest pointing to the right, I had to point my chest to the left so that I could see the ball with my right eye and never take my right eye off the ball. But when I did that, that put me in a slice position. I have designed a new set of clubs here, a driver and some fairway woods, I want you to look at."

"That's very nice," he said. "Why are you telling me this?"

"I want you to put your name on these clubs and have Spalding put them out so as to help the majority of the people playing golf, because I understand that 98 percent of the people are right-eyed. If that is so, and they are trying to play like you, a left-eyed person, did, don't you think we should do something about that?"

"Yeah, something should be done about that."

"Well, why don't you get Spalding to put these clubs out with your name on them?"

"I don't know if I can do that."

"Why not?"

"Well, Spalding has a lot of things in the wind right now. But I'll tell you what. I'll take this up with them and I'll let you know in two weeks."

Within two weeks I got a letter from him, and in the letter he said, "Fred, Spalding says that 'this could be a controversial subject. It could bring on something that we would have to defend, and it would take a great deal of promotion.'

We've got some things in the wind, and Spalding has just said, 'We just can't do it. It could be great, but we are doing very well right now and we don't want to upset the apple cart.' "

Bobby's last paragraph to me said, "Bobby, I think you've got a great idea here. I would suggest that you put them out yourself and see what will happen in trying them out with the people. Carry on with your idea."

I wrote him back and said, "Bobby, I'm disappointed that I couldn't get you and Spalding behind it, but I'll do the best that I can. And thanks very much for your consideration."

I put them out and had good luck with slicers. I got quite a few people to buy the club, but I couldn't put enough promotion behind it. It really didn't work.

So how was my club different? The club we were all familiar with was set with the clubface about an inch to the left of the hosel, and the farther forward that you put the surface that hits the ball (the clubface), the easier it is to slice. So what I did was pull the hitting surface back more in line with the left-hand side of the hosel, which was quite different from what was being manufactured. In so doing, it was such a change that (noted golf expert) George Fazio said to me, "Fred, you've got a good idea here, but you've taken it too far. You should have gradually brought it back." That was kind of upheld when a fellow by the name of Adams came out with what we called a Pittsburgh persimmon club, a steel-shafted club with a metal head. He called it a driver that you could hit off the fairway, so now you had a driver that you could hit off the tee as well as a driver that you could hit off the fairway. It oughtta allow you to hit the ball farther on the par-fives and the long par-fours.

All he did was put twelve degrees of loft on the driver,

and sure enough, you could get the ball off the fairway with it and they were better off the tee. It was just like hitting a three- or two-wood off the tee today instead of the driver. This was just like the design that I had used, and he (Adams), too, had brought his face back there in line, and that was the first fellow who had done the same thing that I had done. Later, I found out that some clubs that were probably used before Harry Vardon were quite comparable to it, but they weren't exactly the same thing. What I had come up with was a club difficult to slice with. It was kind of like a five-iron, which you really can't slice. You can hook the heck out of it, but you do it by closing the face.

---

*Golfer **Paul Runyan** talks a bit about Jones's role-model status in the eyes of young golfers in those days:*

I can't be sure that every youngster in those days wanted to be just like Bobby Jones, but I would imagine that that was the case. One thing about Jones was that he let his clubs do his talking for him. But he was not a great, outgoing figure like a Walter Hagen or a Sam Snead. He was a quiet, gentlemanly Southern player. But I understand that as a youngster he had been a brat. He was so good at such a young age that, so I've been told, during one of his matches Bobby threw his tam-o'-shanter (golf cap) down and stomped on it. And some great British professional he was playing with pushed him aside and said, "Young man, why don't you let me do that. I can do a much a better job of it." And he tore the cap all to pieces, and I think it was because of that incident that Jones never threw any tantrums on the golf course again. During his playing days as a grownup, Jones emerged as the epitome of sportsmanship. His game remained magnificent, even after he retired following his grand slam (in 1930), such as his winning that Augusta Open by so many shots.

———————

Louise Suggs, who played many rounds of golf with Jones over the years, mostly at East Lake Country Club in Atlanta, describes Jones in such a way that makes him sound somewhat like a big brother to her, or perhaps a favorite uncle:

Jones was one of the nicest men I have ever known. I remember one time when I was first getting to know him he walked up to me and said, "Hello, my name is Bob Jones." And I said, "Mr. Jones, if you think everybody in Atlanta doesn't know who you are, then you have rocks in your head." He was a perfect gentleman. It just so happens, too, that he and my mother, Margarite (Spiller Suggs), were the exact same age.

He was very supportive of the development of women's golf as well. One time we held the Titleholders Tournament in Augusta (at Augusta Country Club), and he made arrangements to be there so that he could help present the trophy in committee. Also, about the time we were trying to get the LPGA started, he helped make arrangements for Marilynn Smith, Mary Lena Faulk, and me to meet some people at Augusta, and it happened to be during the week of the Masters Tournaments, and he made sure to get us tickets and all that kind of stuff along with it.

Later I was playing in an LPGA tournament up in Boston when I heard that he had gone into the hospital to have surgery on his neck. I called down there and talked to his wife, Mary. It was just in little ways like that that we kept in touch over the years; some of it wasn't planned, some of it was.

Not many women had the opportunities or inclination to play golf at the time I was starting out. But the opportunity was practically ready-made for me. Because my father owned a public golf course, it was at my back door. That course is no longer there—it could be a shopping center now for all I know. But young women for the most part did not play golf in those days—only the very wealthy, so to speak, who had golf clubs at their disposal. I played in the local tournaments and in Florida during the winter, and then the war came along at about the time. There was no gas, and golf balls were being recycled just like tires were. There wasn't anything to do. So I practiced a lot, just kind of messing around. We knew who Bobby Jones was, but then again, he was just a club member and sometimes we got to play golf with him. He was one of the members and people adored him, but they left him alone.

He had a lot of influence on my game. In fact, I tried to do everything that he did as far as swinging the club was concerned. It's hard to describe, to put into words. Simply put, I was enamored of the way he hit the ball. I still have a compilation of his films that was put together, and several years ago my nephew, Joel Suggs, was watching it and he said, "You did copy his swing, didn't you?" I used to watch him practice a lot, and it was fascinating because it seemed like he never missed a shot. I always went past parallel on my backswing, like he had, even though I don't know if that was really in my mind. I was just trying to do what he did, and as long as you don't lose a ball, it doesn't make any difference where it goes, as far as I am concerned. I wish I could still get back there now, except that I'm now as stiff as a board and there's no way to do it. I would do a little stretching before hitting practice balls, but we didn't know as much about that kind of stuff as they do now. We didn't have these stretching bands and trainers like they do now, although my father, being a ballplayer, knew a little bit about it. But there were no particular exercises prescribed for us.

Herbert Warren Wind was one of golf's most renowned scribes during the mid-twentieth century and is perhaps best remembered as Ben Hogan's collaborator in the authorship of Hogan's perennially best-selling Five Fundamentals *book. Wind made his mark in writing soon after Jones retired from competitive golf in 1930, although Wind had the opportunity to rub shoulders with Jones dozens of times over the years, most frequently during Masters week in April every year:*

As the most popular Southerner since Robert E. Lee and the most admired American athlete in the so-called Golden Age of Sport, (Jones) knew the best that life has to offer, and over the past twenty years (circa 1950 to his death in 1971) he has known some of the worst. He has stood up to both situations with equal grace. He is the only person I know, in or out of sports, who has the Churchillian quality of being larger than life and at the same time intensely human and intimate. I love to be in his company and listen to him talk golf.[9]

Sam Snead's smooth, rhythmic golf swing often has been compared to Jones's, but there is a part of Jones's game that Snead wishes he hadn't emulated, at least later in his career:

My velvet swing hasn't left me, but putting has always been my weak spot—from the word go. Early on I'd modeled myself on Bob Jones, letting my wrists guide my stroke. That's fine when you're young and you've got your nerves. But when you get a few years past thirty, "little things" begin to slip, the same little things that help you win golf tournaments.[10]

THE LEGACY

The legacy of Bobby Jones is multilayered. It begins with his great record as a golfer, all achieved as an amateur. Amateur golf was the foundation of twentieth-century golf in America, buoyed by the memorable victories of Francis Ouimet in the 1913 U.S. Open and Jones in his many major victories, starting with the 1923 U.S. Open. Soon after Jones's retirement from competitive golf in 1930, golf's pro tour started to take off with the burgeoning careers of marquee stars-to-be Sam Snead, Byron Nelson, Gene Sarazen, Ben Hogan, and others. Jones did his part to keep the fires of amateurism stoked, building into the Masters' invitational criteria numerous qualifying spots for amateurs. Although the number of amateurs invited today to the Masters has dwindled, there still is significant recognition given at each year's tournament to low amateur in the field. Jones's legacy is that a golfer who doesn't (or doesn't yet) make a living at golf deserves a special place in golf.

Another of Jones's legacies is the enduring appeal of Augusta National and the Masters Tournament, which have taken on companion cult status ranking somewhere on the prestige meter between a royal wedding and a presidential inauguration. Although devised by Jones and Roberts as the most private of clubs with a golf-course design reeking of hickory-shafted traditionalism, Augusta has become a pop-culture phenomenon open to the world for one week every year. In just seventy years Augusta National has caught up with hundreds-of-years-old St. Andrews in terms of what constitutes a shrine, complete with stone bridges and the whispering ghosts of brokenhearted contenders.

Although Jones passed away in 1971, at age sixty-nine, he lives on at Augusta in one respect: he is the president-in-perpetuity of Augusta National Golf Club.

—⁂—

When **Lionel Hebert** won the 1957 PGA Championship, defeating Dow Finsterwald, 2&1, in the match-play final, he became the last man to win the PGA played in a match-play format. His brother, Jay, would win the PGA three years later. Hebert belonged to a generation of golfers old enough to have known Jones on the level of being part of an acquaintance renewed once a year during Masters week, but too young to have known and played alongside Jones the golfer. That means Hebert's golfing career has touched the likes of Nelson and Hogan on one end and Nicklaus and Palmer on the other. That's the perspective from which Hebert takes a stab at defining where Bobby Jones stands in golf history, which he enriches by offering some of his own background on how he got into golf:

It's hard to evaluate these kinds of things in one part of the century to the other, but golf was totally an unknown sport in this country around the time that Jones was starting to win championships.

I was born in 1928, and I started hanging around the golf course about 1936. I would go to the golf course but I was too small to carry a bag. Eventually I became a caddie. Those were the days where Snead and all of the guys were just starting out. You knew their names because you would go to a movie on a Sunday or Saturday night and the newsreels would show Jones, and Snead, and Hogan, and Nelson playing a golf tournament someplace. I admired those guys. They were superstars in those days. To think that I would get to know them all over the next twenty-five to thirty years was an amazing feat for me, you know.

I played in Jones's tournament something like fourteen times. I didn't get to attend many of the functions with him, but I heard so many great stories. The man was brilliant. He had a brilliant mind, he must have had five or six degrees. He never did turn pro, but in his time, the better golfers were amateurs.

I got to know those guys like Snead, Hogan, and Nelson over the years, and of course they learned a lot of their skills from Jones. You had Jones and then you had Hagen. I didn't play golf with Hagen, but I got to know him a little bit—had a few drinks with him. What a character he was. He was a professional, and Jones was an amateur. Jones was a great example in showing us how to play. How he learned how to play, I don't know.

One golfer that got to know Jones well was Louise Suggs. She grew up in Atlanta, and her daddy was a ballplayer. She played a lot of golf with Jones, when she was a really young person. She had a classic golf swing, doing everything the way he, Jones, did it. Jones had a great influence on the pros.

Look at the equipment he had. Wooden shafts. There was no such thing as a firm shaft back then. In those days if you got a set of clubs with pretty good shafts, you never got rid of them. You had to make your talents fit the club; your clubs didn't fit you. With the wooden shafts, you had to develop a smooth, round swing. When you looked at those old swings, you saw smoothness, timing, and rhythm. They had to play that way because of the golf club. And look at the golf balls they had to play with in those days. They just weren't very good compared to the balls they now use.

I never got to play with Jones, but I watched a lot of film over the years. The first time I got to play in the Masters was in 1956, and he was already in a wheelchair by then. Jay (Hebert) got to know him pretty well. I got to know Jones from a distance. I think he was very intelligent and from what I heard, he didn't put up with a lot of foolishness. But I think he had a good sense of humor, like all Southerners have. He had that Southern drawl, and it was fun just listening to that.

Former CBS-TV golf maestro **Frank Chirkinian** *was there in his director's chair to see the twilight of Ben Hogan's career, the ascensions of Arnold Palmer and Jack Nicklaus to superstardom, and the introductions of the likes of Ben Crenshaw, Tom Watson, Seve Ballesteros, and Nick Price to the winners' circle at Augusta. Chirkinian never saw Jones compete, but he knew enough about Jones and what he brought to the game to offer his* *own assessment of where Jones stood among golf's all-time great champions:*

I have not seen any tickertape parades in New York for Tiger Woods yet. Hogan was the only other golfer, that I can recall, that ever had a tickertape parade. As far as Jones's place in golf is concerned? His story, of course, is going to preserve his image and what he did for the game. You know how quickly fame seems to disappear. It doesn't take long once you are out of the public's image to be pretty much forgotten. I don't think that will ever happen to Bob Jones. I think the mystique of Bob Jones should really live forever. There have been books that have been written, for instance, *The Legend of Bagger Vance*, that still have an angle that has something to do with Bob Jones.

As an aside, one of the reasons I got into trouble in Augusta, at one point, was that I suggested that they change the closing presentation and take it out of the catacombs of the Butler Cabin. My suggestion was to take it up to the area of the practice putting green, where everybody could see it and it wouldn't be that closed, stilted presentation that we always ended up with. At the time, I thought the reason most people stuck around to watch the closing presentation was because of the attraction of the mystique of Bob Jones. Then after '70 or '71, when we had a change in the personnel for the closing presentation (when Jones was removed from the made-for-TV presentation), which was something that was kind of ugly and CBS was blamed for removing Bob Jones—which wasn't true at all. That was Cliff Roberts's work, but he conveniently blamed us for it. The day that I went to see him (Jones) and Mary, his wife, was standing at the steps of the cottage in tears and asking me how I could

137

do such a thing. I said, "I have no idea what you are talking about, Mary. Do what?" Then she told me, and I said, "I'm sorry but that is not true—we had nothing to do with that." She said, "I knew it. I know who did it." We all knew who did it.

Bob Jones Jr. gives some pointers to his son, Bob Jones III, in 1941 before young Bobby makes his debut in competitive golf at Chattanooga, Tennessee, in the Southern Prep and High School Tourney. (AP/Wide World Photos)

The attraction with the closing presentation was the fact that it had always been with Bob Jones. After he left, we had a series of fill-ins for him. I just thought the whole thing went flat. Theatrically, it wasn't acceptable. Here you have just come off this magnificent high, with a winner putting out at eighteen, the adrenaline is flowing, and all of a sudden we bring things to a crashing halt by going into the Butler Cabin. The great thing about Augusta National is how it adheres to tradition. God bless them for that. This is something that we sorely need to maintain and perpetuate. They do it quite well. I can see their viewpoint. I can understand where they're coming from. It is just that as the television producer, I just thought that it just lacked the theatrical necessities to make this thing (the traditional green jacket ceremony in the Butler Cabin) important.

Bob Goalby experienced the Jones mystique as a frequent player in the Masters, including winning the event in 1968. He also was well aware of the mystique that surrounded fellow golfer Ben Hogan, with whom Goalby played more than thirty rounds over the years. Jones and Hogan each emanated a powerful sense of mystique that Goalby tries to explain and compare, along the way offering some insight into why Augusta was set up the way it was, with Jones assisting Dr. Alister Mackenzie in the design and layout of Augusta National:

The Jones mystique was almost like Hogan's, perhaps even more so. There was a real mystique about him. I know that everyone who was a peer of mine in going to Augusta was almost scared of Jones. Some of the awe about Augusta was because Jones was there. Everything about Augusta was Jones, like "Jones did this" or "Jones did that" or "That's why Jones built this" or "That's why Jones did that." With Hogan I was still in double awe, but I got to play with him quite a few times (thirty-one), so I was probably more in awe with Jones, a guy I never got to play with. I remember all I had the first year I played the tour was, "the Masters, the Masters, the Masters. You'll play it good because you have the kind of game that will play there." One time some of us guys were in a car driving from Oklahoma City to Hot Springs, and Doug Ford was in the car and told me every hole, every shot I was going to play, and everything I was going to do, and it was in 1959 when I was going to go. No other tournament did we do something like that. I got to know Hogan a little bit better and got to eat lunch with him.

I've heard that Jones wasn't a real straight driver and that's why he wanted a little room at Augusta. He believed that the focus should be on the second shot and the play on and around the green. Being a good putter and a good chipper is perhaps why he did that. Nicklaus builds golf courses a little wider off the tee than most, because Jack likes to be able to bomb it and play golf, although he will tighten it down and make it difficult going into the green. I think that's the best way to be. I hate to see these public courses where the average hacker is in a bunker off the tee on every hole, where he can't even play. That's no fun and it hurts the game—it takes too long to play and then people are disgusted, saying, "I'm not going to follow that game up anymore." At Augusta, they can make the course as hard as they want by the pin placements because the greens border on unfair at times, depending on where you put the pins. But if you put the pins in the middle where the greens aren't quite as fast, then the course becomes almost easy. Members there shoot pretty good scores, and people who have come in and played it can't believe how hard it can get during the tournament. But if they played from the back tees with the fast greens and the hard pin placements, they would find out, ha ha. They would find out quick.

———————

Goalby, whose career overlapped Hogan's and Nicklaus's, offers his assessment of where Jones ranks in the annals of golf history and its great champions from different eras:

I've always thought a champion in one era would be a champion in another era. Some will say, "Well, he (e.g., Jones) didn't hit it as far" or whatever, but my thought is if they were living in this day and age, they would be hitting just as far as the long hitters now. If they were long then, they would be long now. They would be just as good, maybe even better when you add in all the money that's available now.

There's no doubt in my mind that Jones stacks up with the best of them, the top three or four. With Tiger (Woods), we still don't know. He's damn good, we know that. He's fantastic. He's got a great grip, a good setup, a good swing, perfect plane, he's smart, he's strong and tall, and he's confident as hell. And he can putt like crazy. He's got all the ingredients. He could disappear just by desire or something, but I think he's worked too hard to get there to want to go away. Jones apparently accomplished all he thought he could do and maybe he got tired of tournament golf. You know, a lot of people get tired early. People like Curtis Strange, too. My nephew (Jay Haas) won the National Peewee at age eight.

Well, he's forty-seven now and didn't play much this past year (2000). I think people get burned out.

---

*Jones wasn't just a pioneer as a great champion heightening American interest in the sport, he also was a visionary of sorts. When Jones was still competing, as an amateur, the only golfers playing for money as pros were regarded as one notch above gypsies. If a golfer had a college degree, more than nine times out of ten he pursued a career away from golf and continued to compete only as time, resources, and desire allowed. Amateurs, for the most part, were the best golfers because there really was very little money to be made at golf competition. Still, even with that kind of background, Jones had the foresight to see that the future of golf growth in America was a pro tour dominated by former college players, which otherwise was an alien concept in those days. College graduates gravitating to the pro golf circuit? Preposterous! But think: In helping to design Augusta National, Jones could see what the course would look like fifty or sixty years later, when trees had grown to their full height, gradually changing the landscape over the years and thus changing the way many of the holes could be played. He was a visionary. Likewise, as **Freddie Haas** suggests, Jones by the thirties and forties was seeing golf as a sport whose future would depend largely on college graduates, or at least college golfers:*

I think I got to know Bobby real well. He talked to me at length without charging legal fees and he gave me some marvelous advice over the years about things like clubs and my game. He encouraged me to play, and he said, "We need fellows who have won the intercollegiate to get into golf." We need college golfers, which I thought was thinking ahead of its time because at the time I got into golf I think there were only two guys other than Jones who had gone to college, including Lawson Little, and then (Cary) Middlecoff followed me. Colleges then started getting golf scholarship programs, and the college golfers started getting so good that they weren't being allowed to play in their local tournaments anymore, and they pretty much had to turn pro to find the competition. That was the start of the college crowd getting into pro golf.

Jones didn't have anything to do with us college players turning pro; he just encouraged us to get as good as we could. And the schools wanted us to be good so they could win the intercollegiate championships. In this sense Bobby was a visionary, knowing that college golfers would be so much a future of the game. When I sat next to him in 1938 during a Walker Cup sendoff ceremony, he thought that getting college golfers into the game would not only improve the character of the players who end up playing on the tour, but it will also improve the quality of play. He was all sold on the idea that you would get a good education in school and that when you then came out on tour it would make for a better tour.

Up until that time, you had people like Walter Hagen, whose drinking I think was exaggerated and a few other people who, shall we say, played their own game, who comprised the golf tour. Now you have a different breed of cat out there. You've got well-educated guys who can really play the game of golf. That's not bad.

Doug Ford has this to say in analyzing Jones's place in golf history:

He had a great influence on the game. I don't think the impact he had at that time was as great as it became until after he stopped playing. In America, players started coming out of the Northeast and then it changed out to the South and then to Texas and then to California, where a lot of the players started coming from. I would have to rate him among the top five players of all time just on his tournament record, but I think that Snead's the greatest player who ever played. But then you talk to Snead and he'll tell you how great Byron Nelson was. And I thought Hogan might have been a better player than Nelson, but then again, I only saw Nelson after he had retired from tournament golf. I had played with Hogan when he was at his best. But Snead still, to me, could hit the best shots and he could hit all the shots.

———

Doug Ford offers his thoughts on the Mystique Factor when comparing Jones to Hogan:

I say the edge goes to Jones because there was no television in his day. He was a newspaper phenom in the sense that you had to read about him to know about him, and yet he has such a prominent place in history. A lot of it is because of the media and the way things are handled now. The less exposed a guy is, the more mysterious he is.

———

Byron Nelson is another of the select few still around who knew both Jones and Hogan well enough to offer some credible comments about the mystique of the two men, in this case Jones:

From that standpoint of mystique they were somewhat alike. They both had a sense of mystique about them. But Jones's mystique was mainly because of his name and the fact that he hadn't competed for very long. He was also a very shrewd attorney, but he was always willing to talk to anybody at any time. His whole general demeanor was one of friendliness, yet reserve. He had his own opinions about things and didn't mind expressing them, but he never did so unpleasantly. You knew where he stood right away.

Jones really meant so much to golf even after he retired because of the Masters and the things he lent his name to. He did play in a number of his tournaments, but one thing about him is that he was never able to negotiate his own tricky greens very well. But I played with him one time in a practice round in 1942 and he had a 32 on the back nine, and he did it pretty easily. But we were just out playing around that time.

Runyan addresses the so-called Jones mystique and recalls the last few times he saw Jones at Augusta:

I think there was very little mystique about Bobby Jones, unless you're talking about his being quiet and austere. I guess not a lot of people really got to know Bobby Jones very well. The only time I saw him fairly excited was when they had the tickertape parade for him in New York after he won the Grand Slam (in 1930). Otherwise, I never saw him get terribly excited.

The last time I saw him at Augusta, I don't think he weighed more than 110 pounds. He was just skin and bones. He was still smoking too much, but even then his head was clear and we spoke about so many wonderful things that had happened in the past. He still had dreams of accomplishing more things for Augusta National and golf in general. Looking back, I think Jones had more to do with the development of the Masters than Clifford Roberts did, even though Roberts gave his life to it.

Jones had a great impact on the game, but not quite the impact of Arnold Palmer because that wasn't his way; Jones was too quiet and reserved to be like that. But in his quiet, reserved way, he had as much influence as Walter Hagen had had in his flamboyant way. Hagen did more for the professional golfers than any other human being, but it's highly questionable in my mind as to whether Hagen did quite as much for the promotion of the game as did Bobby Jones. I don't think Hagen cared too much about what he did for golf itself; he just played flamboyantly. He had to have the biggest car and the best there was in clothes. He played with a flair and it probably did more to promote Hagen than it did to promote golf, where Jones did more to promote golf and less to promote himself.

As for Jones the golfer, the one thing that stands out for me occurred in the first round of the first Masters (in 1934). We played the course in reverse in those days; that is, we played what is now the tenth hole as the first hole and what is now the first hole as the tenth. On the then-eleventh hole—the second hole now—his drive came to rest on the steepest downslope on the right edge of the fairway. The pin was cut back and to the left, making it the longest possible second shot he could have had from where he was. From off that steep slope, he hit a shot that once it got up in the air I thought, *Oh, my goodness, he's hit it too far. It's going to carry into the bunker in front*, because I had hit my second shot from about thirty yards in back of his and I ended up eighty yards short of the bunker. Well, it didn't stop in the bunker. It carried over the bunker and landed fourteen feet from the hole and rolled to about eighteen or twenty feet behind the hole. I asked him, "What kind of a spoon did you hit that with?" And he said, "Oh, I didn't hit it with my spoon. I hit it with my brassie." Well, to get a ball up in the air with a two-wood from a steep downslope and then to get it far enough to carry the bunker yet getting it to stop on the green was the finest fairway wood shot I had ever seen, before or since, and I've seen a lot of them. I've hit a few of those myself. Any time I wanted to get a shot that would carry and then stop like that, I had to be within 180 yards of the hole. His was about 230 yards from the hole and with a downslope that had to be at least twenty degrees. Just think of the balance you have to have in the first place just to be able to make decent contact with the ball, let alone do with it what he did.

Freddie Haas was one of, essentially, a handful of people still alive at the end of the twentieth century who could claim to be well acquainted with both Bobby Jones and Ben Hogan. If anyone had a sense for the Jones mystique vs. the Hogan mystique, it was Haas, and here's what he says:

Jones had a mystique because he didn't play very much. He was twenty-eight when he retired. He had a legal education and was in such demand, and was so interested in building Augusta National, which took about three or four years, he got to where he just wasn't available very much. Plus the media was covering him only when he was winning the championships. He wasn't an every-week tournament player by any means. He only played three, four, or five times a year after he retired, so he wasn't much to be seen in the media's eyes. People knew he was great and that everything was fine and when they played the Masters, Hooray for Bobby, you know. But other than that, you just didn't see or read much about him. He had some years between the time he retired (1930) and when the Masters started (1934) that he just wasn't in the news hardly at all. When he came out of retirement, that really brought some attention because everyone wanted to know how well he would play against the current crop of great players. It was very interesting and brought on a whole lot of attention, to include (writers) Grantland Rice and O. B. Keeler at the forefront. They did everything they could to promote not only Bobby, but also to promote the game of golf, and in doing so promoted the Augusta National. It was all good press.

As far as Hogan was concerned, he started out—and we all knew he was going to be good—not having the winning ability that Snead, for instance, did. It wasn't until he changed his whole golf game around 1938 did it start to look like he was going to be pretty good. I remember playing with him in a tournament in New Orleans in 1938, and on the first hole he duck-hooked his drive, he duck-hooked his second shot, he duck-hooked his third shot, and the ball rolls up twenty-five feet from the hole and he holes it for a par-four. Well, you can't play golf like that and win. It's going to cause you some trouble.

The next time I saw him was about a year later, and instead of that duck-hook, he was hitting that high slider to the right. I said, "Ben, you've changed your golf game." Ben didn't want to explain very much about what he had done, because he was working this out by himself, I guess. The funny part about it was, I was trying to get out of my hook and trying to hit a high slice, and then I saw him doing it. He finally said, yeah, that he had changed his game, and then he finally gave me an explanation. He said, "Fred, I had to do it. When I played with you, I was hitting that low, ducking hook, and I knew with that I could never stop the ball on the green, particularly if they put the pin behind a trap, a mound, or a water hazard. So I had to completely change over to a high, strong slider (fade)." I said, "Was that for your scoring ability?" And he said, "Yes. The four majors are so difficult to win, that if you can't hit a ball into the green that will stop, you will never be able to win a major. I want to win some majors." I said, "Ben, thank you very much. That's certainly understandable."

I was delighted with his answer because that's what I was trying to do. He perfected it, he really did. From then on, people would say, "You know, I don't know if a hook is the best way to play this game or not."

The other time that I talked to Hogan was after he had two putts from about fifteen to eighteen feet to beat Fred Hawkins in the Colonial National Invitation Tournament in Fort Worth. He lagged the first putt about fifteen to eighteen inches short of the hole. When the time came to putt, he took up a rather unusual stroke and knocked it only about five inches. Now he's left with a one-foot putt and what did he do? He just jabbed at the ball without changing his feet or anything, and it was lucky that the ball went in. Why it went in, I don't know. He was so disgusted with himself for the second putt. The next day he shot 69 to beat Hawkins and win the tournament. I saw him after that, and this was when he gave me a second observation. I said to him, "It looked to me like you had difficulty getting the club back on your putting." He just couldn't pull the trigger. He said, "That's right." And I said, "Would you like an observation?" I just wanted to tell him to do something to put something in motion. You can't do anything just standing there in neutral. He said, "No, I don't want to know. Fred, I appreciate your concern, but I don't want to be remembered for just being a great putter. I want to be remembered as the greatest striker of the ball." I said to myself, Well, this guy wants to win, but that's not his main goal. His main goal is to be able to do with the ball whatever it is he wants done with it. I think he played that way, and not too many other people did.

Hogan just didn't want to get involved with other people. I liked to play with him, whereas someone like Lloyd Mangrum felt ill at ease playing with him. I felt great when I played with Hogan because he played his game and allowed you to play yours. A lot of the other fellows wouldn't do that. They would always be fidgeting or moving at the wrong time or standing in the wrong place—they interfered with your game. Ben Hogan did not, but Ben wouldn't talk to Lloyd Mangrum when they were playing, either. Can you imagine if (Lee) Trevino had ever played with Hogan? That would have really been something.

Hogan and Jones were exact opposites, except that they both started out being left-handers—left-eyed and hooking the ball, and Hogan was able to overcome it and Jones was not. They adopted different methods to achieve success. Bobby played with his chest back, and he had a different swing—he even had a little loop in his swing, that when he had it under control, he was really great. When he didn't have it under control near the end there, he was really pitiful. In terms of personality, Jones had more interests than Hogan. Hogan was totally immersed in golf, and when he cut back, he went into the Hogan golf club business. Jones put out golf clubs only in the sense that he put his name on the clubs that Spalding put out—he didn't really have anything to do with them. Hogan inspected every club that went through his factory, and the first batch that came through he threw them all out and told his people, "You've got to do better than this." He took an active interest in building golf clubs, but didn't have much interest in doing anything else related to golf such as building golf courses or whatever. He wanted to play the game and come up with golf clubs that were superior to anything else on the market at the time.

Jones had his share of close cronies, but I don't really know who could have called himself a friend of Hogan's. I considered myself an acquaintance of Hogan's—I must have played with him a hundred times in tournaments and thoroughly enjoyed it, but other than those two conversations I had with him there wasn't much else between us. But everybody thought well of him.

I called up Hogan one day when I was doing something with my Freddie Haas putter line, and I asked Ben, "Ben, I've got a line of putters here that I think are outstanding. I haven't seen you come out with a line of putters. Why don't you take this line of putters, make them a part of the Ben Hogan Golf Company, and go with them?" He said, "Fred, I can't do that because I don't put out anything that doesn't have Ben Hogan's name on it." And so that was the end of that.

———

Jones had a tremendous influence on a great many golfers, **Jack Nicklaus** *among them. That Jones influence was part of the impetus that inspired Nicklaus to create Muirfield Village, which was to become the host site for "Jack's tournament," the Memorial. The first Memorial Tournament was played at Muirfield Village Golf Club in Dublin, Ohio, in May 1976. Jones, who had passed away five years earlier after a long illness, was the Memorial's first honoree. Nicklaus reminisces:*

In preparation for the tournament, I had prevailed on friends who had served golf notably in one or another capacity to become members of an entity we named the Captains Club, principally to select our honoree each year, but also to provide general counsel on tournament policy and operations. Much to my delight, they had selected Bob Jones as our first honoree; and the first of what has become a popular pre-tournament ceremony, beautifully emceed by Joe Dey, went off gracefully in a lovely setting behind the eighteenth green. Bob's grandson and daughter-in-law attended, along with his partner in the creation of Augusta National and the Masters, Clifford Roberts, wearing the gray blazer of a Captains Club member. Mr. Roberts had first paid a visit to Muirfield Village in the fall of 1974, then written me a letter in which he said, "You have a chance to do there in five years what it took us forty years to accomplish in Augusta." He mentioned this again the day we honored Bob, and it was a personal highlight of an altogether happy week.[1]

——————

One golfer whose career was long enough to give him firsthand exposure to the golf games of both Bobby Jones and Jack Nicklaus is **Sam Snead,** *who was still consistently shooting well below his age when he was in his eighties:*

I played two exhibitions with Bobby Jones and one round at Augusta. He was a good driver of the ball and a good fairway-woods player. And he was probably the best putter of his era. But he wasn't as good with his long irons. Yet, Jack Nicklaus was never a great sand or wedge player. But he hit it a long way, and I think Jack was the best putter there ever was.

——————

Arnold Palmer, *golfing hero to millions, had his own heroes and one of them was, of course, Bob Jones. From Jones, Palmer drew many lessons about golf, but one of the things he took from Jones was some advice that helped him deal with the painful loss of his best friend Bud Worsham, a Wake Forest pal of his that was killed in a car crash in 1950:*

Bob Jones, my first golf hero, once commented that he never learned anything from a golf tournament he won. It may sound absurd to compare the death of my best friend to losing a golf tournament, but I've learned life really does resemble a golf round in its crazy ups and downs. For better or

It is 1930 and Jones is flanked on his right by inventor C. Francis Jenkins and on his left by PGA officer George Sargent. They surround a new, innovative camera with a shutter speed of 3,200 frames a second, which would be used to photograph Jones's swings for instructional purposes. (AP/Wide World Photos)

worse, those moments of unaccountable loss or failure teach us the most about who we are, where we've come from, and where we may be headed.[2]

Although Jones was already ten years retired from competitive golf before **Jack Nicklaus** *was born, Nicklaus developed a powerful appreciation for Jones at an early age because of the influence of Nicklaus's father, Charlie, who years earlier had watched Jones win the 1926 U.S. Open, held at "next-door"*

Scioto Country Club in Columbus, Ohio. Jack Nicklaus would finally meet his and his dad's idol in 1955:

The impact of this (Charlie Nicklaus's idolatry of Jones) on me was that seemingly every time, as a youngster, Dad and I talked seriously about some aspect of golf, Bob Jones would come up in one form or another. Also, Jack Grout (Nicklaus's golf coach for many years) had known Jones well and admired him greatly and, like Dad, loved to reminisce about both his wonderful golf and his fine personal qualities. The result was that, by the time I first met Jones, he had become a heroic figure to me. So far as I tried to emulate anyone in my early teens, he was the man.

The occasion of our first meeting was the 1955 National Amateur, played at the James River course of the Country Club of Virginia. Mr. Jones had been invited by the United States Golf Association to speak at the traditional prechampionship players' dinner on this, the twenty-fifth anniversary of his Amateur victory at Merion that completed his 1930 Grand Slam. At fifteen, I was the youngest player in the field. During a practice round, Bob had seen me get home in two at the 460-yard eighteenth hole and asked to meet me. Both Dad and I found him easy and pleasant to talk to. Finally he told me, "Young man, there were only a couple of fellas who got home on that hole today and you were one of them. I'm going to come out and watch you play some more tomorrow."

. . . All through the first nine the next day I'm looking over my shoulder for Bobby Jones, and finally I see him coming down the tenth fairway in his golf cart as I'm getting ready to tee up at number eleven. At that point I'm one up in the match and feeling pretty good about myself. Half an hour later I'm two down, having gone bogey, bogey, double-bogey. Whereupon Bob Jones turns to Dad, who's walking with us, and says, "I don't believe I'm doing young Jack much good. I think I'd better get out of here." Which he does. Right away I get back to even, but then bogey the last hole to lose the match one down.

As he later explained to my father, Bob felt that his presence might have started me trying too hard, and thus took off as soon as he could without, he hoped, leaving us with the feeling that he had given up on me too quickly. Even at that minimally perceptive age, I was impressed by such sensitivity to and concern for a youngster with whom he had made only the most casual acquaintance. As our friendship deepened over the years, it was for me this kind of thoughtfulness and graciousness to everyone he encountered that continued to shine brightest of his many qualities.[3]

Jones's retirement from the amateur ranks was made in a manner typical of the man. He might well have evaded the letter of the amateur rule and still made the educational motion pictures that lured him beyond the pale of amateurism. But with the same inherent honesty that made him call numerous penalty strokes, on himself, in the heat of championships he preferred to sacrifice his amateur standing—which he always guarded with tremendous jealousy—rather than violate the tenets of the class. In his retirement, Jones has given another example of the same splendid sportsmanship he so often exhibited on the fairways.[4]

This is one of the many things that Jones had to say, in general, on how this great game is to be regarded:

It seems to me that there are two reasonable ways in which a man may take his golf. If he has the time and inclination to do so, he may set out to give the game a proper amount of serious study and effort, with a view toward elevating himself beyond the average-golfer class; or, if he has only a very limited amount of free time, as many have, he may be content to knock around with his regular companions who play about as he does, in search of a little fun. But it will not do to mix the two, especially to hang the ambitions of the first man upon the labors of the latter.[5]

———

*If Jones was the greatest amateur in the history of the game, his rival of sorts, **Walter Hagen,** has a spot in history as the true American pioneer of professional golf. Until well into the 1930s, golf, at least golf in America, was a sport for amateurs. Professionals for the most part were viewed somewhat as charlatans for violating the spirit of the game, performing for money almost as if part of some kind of carnival. But as flamboyant as Hagen was as America's best-known golf pro, he also had a deep love and appreciation for the game. Throughout most of the 1920s, Hagen and Jones operated in parallel universes—Hagen as America's No. 1 pro and Jones as America's darling amateur. Their worlds finally collided in a seventy-two-hole exhibition match that was arranged in 1926. Hagen ended up winning decisively, 12&11, in a match that he later looked back upon in his own memoirs:*

I was not eager for the match for a number of reasons. Inasmuch as the papers said he was the better of the two of us, I'd have everything to gain and nothing to lose. But I was not keen on taking a beating from him. Having won my second PGA title that year, my stock was selling pretty high. I couldn't see how a possible defeat at Jones's hands would increase its value. Besides, I was busy having a good time in Florida, and I wasn't interested in interrupting the routine. What is more, Bobby, acknowledged the leading medalist in golf, was the Amateur champion of the United States, and the public somehow had come to consider the amateurs as the Galahads of golf. While I, rated as the leading match player, was a professional—the natural villain of the game. . . .

Although in our challenge match I was successful in defeating Bobby Jones, I believe his attitude toward the game . . . his quiet, cool, analytical type of play was more disconcerting to me than the explosive, erratic temperament of many other golfers. However, his game in our particular match wasn't at its best.[6]

Freddie Haas has lived long enough to see about four or five generations of golfers go by, and he puts Jones at the head of the class in terms of popularizing golf in America, in effect laying the foundation for thousands of others who came behind him:

My guess is that he carried on where Francis Ouimet left off. Ouimet's beating Vardon and Ted Ray at the 1913 U.S. Open was a tremendous impetus for the development of the game in America. Bobby Jones just followed through with his victories and conquests, and he exhibited an overall demeanor that was just really outstanding. He was really the idol of all of us. It was such an honor to get invited to the Masters, and there's no question it was Bobby Jones who made the tournament. He even played in the first few and stayed with it for such a long time. He never did play well in the tournament, though. His hook just killed him, even though the golf course—except for the eighteenth hole—favored a hook.

Everybody thought at that time, at least in the early days of Augusta and the Masters, that the best shot to hit—anywhere, on any golf course, regardless—was a hook. A slice was not a good thing at all. The Augusta National golf course was set up in such a way as to favor a golfer who could hook the ball and putt well, and if you won that tournament, everyone thought you should be able to win every other tournament. Not one player I know of who was outstanding turned down an invitation until Lee Trevino said he couldn't play a hook at that golf course, because he wanted to hit the ball straight or work it left to right. It just wasn't his cup of tea. Everyone else had just fought it the best they could and didn't say anything. They were just delighted to be invited back if they could.

The course was a demonstration of Jones's personality, for sure. But don't forget, in those early years everyone thought the way Jones played was the only right way to play. So everybody tried to hit a hook. Let me tell you something, us right-handed guys can't play too well with a hook. Sooner or later you had to accommodate the right-eyed guy, and they are doing it somewhat these days, but not quite as much as they can because it still isn't understood and certainly isn't anything taught by the PGA. Maybe people will disagree with me, but the first thing I ask people when I am trying to teach them is, Are you right- or left-handed? Do you write with your left hand or with your right? Do you pick up a glass with your left hand or your right hand to get a drink? Those are things that if you can naturally do, you can do better than by forcing yourself or training yourself to do something that's not natural for you.

———

Louise Suggs, *a founding member of the LPGA Hall of Fame as well as the first woman ever inducted into the Georgia Athletic Hall of Fame, credits Jones, one of her early mentors, as being one of the most important figures in the emergence of golf in America as a major sport:*

I think he's the beginning of golf as we now see it in the United States. It has done nothing but gone up since his day. What he did, even by today's standards, is mind-boggling. The set of clubs he played with, those wooden-shafted clubs, were clubs that he had chosen individually in piecing together a set. Sometime later his clubs were tested for swing weight and they were almost perfectly balanced. That's the kind of feel that the man had. That's what golf is—a game of feel and touch; hand-eye coordination. There never has been a truer description.

In Atlanta, because of him, we had a great golfing community. There were many young people, and I would have been about the youngest of them, who all grew up together. The Yates brothers, Charlie and Danny. Tommy Barnes and his brother. Dot Kirby and me. We were both national champions by our early twenties. We all ran into Jones at one time or another, and we all were able to play a few holes with him occasionally. We all played together occasionally, pickup type stuff. We called ourselves the Georgia Golf Mafia. At least that's what I always called it. There must have been about fifteen or twenty of us. We all became champions of one sort or another. There were quite a few new courses opening up in Georgia at the time and we were able to help dedicate them. We were just part of a group that played golf. It was because of him that a lot of us played. I played because my dad owned a golf course, but a lot of the others played because they saw Jones at the club, and he was somebody to admire and emulate. He was very quiet as a rule—a very soft-spoken man. Just an all-around good guy. There was no set routine or protocol for playing with him. Heck, you might run into him on a street somewhere and he would ask you if you wanted to go play.

I played Augusta National a couple of times, but never got to play it with him. I could play there whenever I was in town. I would just call him up and he would arrange it for me. In those days they couldn't give Masters tickets away for people to go out and watch it. I would sometimes get to play the course the day after the tournament, when the cups were left the same as they had been the day before. I remember the first time I was at the tournament and I tried to enter the clubhouse, when one of the Pinkerton guards stopped me and said, "Ma'am, I know who you are, but do you have a badge?" That was the first time I had ever been so questioned. Heck, there weren't even that many people around. I guess that was in the late forties. In playing the course, I remember it being in immaculate shape compared to anything else I had ever played. The greens were fast but not as fast as they are now.

And the course has been changed since those days. I shot in the middle seventies on it.

———⟨⟩———

John Derr, for many years one of CBS-TV's most popular golf announcers, has been around golf and the Masters long enough to have been at Augusta National in 1935 when Gene Sarazen struck the shot heard 'round the world—a fairway-wood second shot at the fifteenth hole that dropped for a double bogey and, in effect, allowed Sarazen to force a playoff with Craig Wood, which Sarazen won the next day. In his book Uphill Is Easier, *Derr portrays Jones as a genuine American sports hero who transcended his sport and his era:*

It was my good fortune to have lived during the middle of the twentieth century when, even without the benefit of television, America produced a number of sports heroes who were bigger than life. A myriad of sportswriters helped make it so. These were great athletes, judged by their performances.

One such hero was Robert Tyre Jones Jr. of Atlanta, Georgia, known to an admiring public as Bobby Jones, but known to his friends simply as Bob, the name he favored after his youthful days. If you ever encounter someone who tells you he was a good friend of "Bobby Jones," look askance on that friendship.

The records Jones set in golf, the tournaments he won and his dominance of the world golf scene for two decades, are all available in record books. They will not be dealt with here.

Spend a few moments of personal recall of Jones, the

man. I was at the second Masters (1935) that as a young sportswriter I met him. Grantland Rice, the best-known sportswriter of that era, whom I had met the day before, asked if I had met Mr. Jones. When I said I hadn't, Mr. Rice, himself a charming, kindly soul, found an opportunity to introduce me.

A friendship begun that day continued throughout his life. Through that acquaintanceship many doors were opened for me and many important sports heroes were met. I never knew why Bob "took a liking" to me, but I respected him being my friend.

Some years later Bob was being given an award by the Metropolitan Golf Writers Association in a New York hotel; and prior to the dinner I was visiting with him in the reception room. As we were talking, a large, graying man, with the look of an old athlete written in his manner of walking, came across the room to our side of the hall.

"Do you recognize that fellow?" Jones asked me.

I didn't.

By that time he had reached us, obviously coming to greet the honored guest.

"Shake hands with Ty Cobb." Bob's simple introduction . . . so typical of Jones's thoughtfulness, this kind, caring man. As the two sons of Georgia exchanged pleasantries, I couldn't help but think how different were these two dominant sportsmen, each recognized as the best in his field . . . one universally loved and one whose great career had generated intense hatred.

Twice I had the thrill of having Jones ask me to lend him my good right arm. The first time was at the funeral of his good friend, Grantland Rice. Bob was an honorary pallbearer, one of many. He had come to New York for the funeral, even though his crippling illness already hindered his walking unattended.

That he asked my help in walking up the aisle thrilled me. Another pallbearer would have been pleased to lend him an arm and that star-studded procession read like a Who's Who. Among them were Jack Dempsey, Eddie Arcaro, Red Blaik, Casey Stengel, Bill Corum, Red Barber, Ted Husing, Elmer Layden, Don Budge, and Hank Greenberg.

They were all all-time greats, except for the young lad on whose right arm Jones laboriously made his way up the aisle.

The other time he asked me to lend him an arm was at Golf House in Manhattan where the USGA was unveiling the likeness of Jones that had been painted by President Eisenhower. It was such a simple act, to assist him to the dais, but to be at his side in this impressive moment of his career was rewarding.

True, I was only his "aisle caddie," but he was My Man.[7]

NOTES

CHAPTER 1: THE ATLANTA CONNECTION

1. Tom Scott and Geoffrey Cousins, *The Golf Immortals* (New York: Hart Publishing Company, 1969), p. 89.

2. Herbert Warren Wind, "Jones Breaks Through," in *Herbert Warren Wind's Golf Book* (New York: Simon and Schuster, 1971), pp. 31–32.

3. Bobby Jones, *Bobby Jones on Golf* (New York: Doubleday, 1963), pp. 14–15.

4. Robert T. Jones Jr. and O. B. Keeler, *Down the Fairway: The Golf Life and Play of Robert T. Jones Jr.* (New York: Minton, Balch, and Company, 1927). Reprinted 1985 by Ailsa, Inc., pp. 32–33.

5. Grantland Rice, from the writings of O. B. Keeler, *The Bobby Jones Story* (Atlanta: Tupper and Love, 1953), pp. 6–7.

165

6. Jones and Keeler, p. 25.
7. Clifford Roberts, *The Story of the Augusta National Golf Club* (Garden City, N.Y.: Doubleday and Company, 1976), p. 158.

CHAPTER 2: GRAND SLAM CHAMPION

1. Herbert Warren Wind, "Jones Breaks Through," in *Herbert Warren Wind's Golf Book*, p. 37.
2. Jones.
3. Jones and Keeler.
4. Ibid., p. 39.
5. Ibid., p. 118.
6. Mark Shaw, *Nicklaus* (Dallas: Taylor Publishing, 1997), p. 340.
7. Roberts, p. 10
8. Jones, p. 5.
9. Ibid., pp. 60, 61.
10. Ibid.
11. Harvey Penick, with Bud Shrake, *Harvey Penick's Little Red Book: Lessons and Teachings from a Lifetime of Golf* (New York: Simon and Schuster, 1992), p. 133.
12. Martin Davis, with Alistair Cooke; Tracey Behar, ed. *Bobby Jones: The Greatest of Them All* (New York: Broadway Books, 1997).
13. Francis J. Powers, "Jones Retires from Competitive Golf," *Golfer's Magazine*, December 1930.
14. Jones, p. 5.
15. Ibid., pp. 101–102.
16. Ibid., p. 114.
17. Penick and Shrake, p. 134.
18. Jones and Keeler, p. 171.

19. Tom Scott and Geoffrey Cousin, *The Golf Immortals* (New York: Hart Publishing Company, 1969), p. 94.

20. Jones and Keeler, pp. 223–225.

21. Reprinted with permission from *Uphill Is Easier: A Reporter's Journal*, by John Derr (Pinehurst, N.C.: Cricket Productions, 1995).

22. Jack Nicklaus, with Ken Bowden, *Jack Nicklaus: My Story* (New York: Fireside, 1997), p. 303.

23. Ibid., pp. 109–110.

24. Sam Snead, with George Mendoza, *Slammin' Sam* (New York: Donald I. Fine, 1986), p. 186.

25. Nicklaus and Bowden, pp. 312–313.

26. Arnold Palmer, with James Dodson, *A Golfer's Life* (New York: Ballantine Books, 1999), pp. 356–357.

27. Reprinted with permission from *Uphill Is Easier: A Reporter's Journal*, by John Derr.

CHAPTER 3: AUGUSTA AND THE MASTERS

1. Roberts, p. 9.

2. Ibid., p. 23.

3. David Owen, *The Making of the Masters: Clifford Roberts, Augusta National, and Golf's Most Prestigious Tournament* (New York: Simon and Schuster, 1999).

4. Roberts, p. 12.

5. Byron Nelson, *How I Played the Game* (Dallas: Taylor Publishing, 1993), pp. 230–231.

6. Roberts, p. 116.

7. Ibid., p. 184.

8. Reprinted with permission from *Uphill Is Easier: A Reporter's Journal*, by John Derr.

Chapter 4: Role Model

1. Owen.
2. Ibid.
3. Davis and Cooke.
4. Herbert Warren Wind, "Jones Breaks Through," in *Herbert Warren Wind's Golf Book*. pp. 34–35.
5. Jones and Keeler, p. 65.
6. Jones, pp. 46–47.
7. Ibid., p. 50.
8. Penick and Shrake, p. 32.
9. Herbert Warren Wind, "The 1968 Masters: Rule 38, Paragraph 3," reprinted in *Herbert Warren Wind's Golf Book*. p. 168.
10. Snead and Mendoza, p. 162.

Chapter 5: The Legacy

1. Nicklaus and Bowden, p. 350.
2. Palmer and Dodson, p. 64.
3. Nicklaus and Bowden, pp. 93-94.
4. Francis J. Powers, "Jones Retires from Competitive Golf."
5. Jones, p. 180.
6. Walter Hagen, as told to Margaret Seaton Heck, *The Walter Hagen Story* (New York: Simon and Schuster, 1956), p. 148.
7. Reprinted with permission from *Uphill Is Easier: A Reporter's Journal*, by John Derr.

INDEX

M

Mackenzie, Alister, 72, 83, 139
Maiden, Stewart, 5–7, 38
Mangrum, Lloyd, 150
McClure, Edwin, 115
Middlecoff, Cary, 104
Miller, Dick, 31

N

Nelson, Byron, 42–45, 70–73, 77–78, 133, 135, 144–145
Nicklaus, Jack, 26–27, 49–52, 53–54, 100, 136, 152–153, 154–156

O

Ouimet, Francis, 133, 158

P

Palmer, Arnold, 56–57, 91, 136, 146, 153–154
Penick, Harvey, 35, 39, 122
Picard, Henry, 46
Player, Gary, 26
Powers, Francis, 36–37
Price, Charles, 28–29, 33–35
Price, Nick, 136

R

Ragsdale, I. W., 11
Revolta, Johnny, 54
Rice, Grantland, 9–10, 29
Roberts, Clifford, 12–13, 31–32, 66–69, 76–77, 85–86, 94, 106, 107–108, 137, 146, 152
Runyan, Paul, 46–48, 58–59, 82–83, 128–129, 145–147

S

Sarazen, Gene, 17, 26, 45, 66, 133
Sargent, George, 154
Scott, Tom, 6, 40
Smith, Horton, 45, 80–81, 117, 123
Smith, MacDonald, 47
Smith, Marilynn, 129
Snead, Sam, 45, 47, 52, 54, 97–98, 105–106, 132, 133, 135, 144, 153
Snider, George, 80–81
Stirling, Alexa, 6, 9
Suggs, Louise, 13–14, 129–131, 135–136, 160–162

About the Author

Mike Towle is a veteran sportswriter and author whose previous books include *The Ultimate Golf Trivia Book*, *I Remember Ben Hogan*, and *I Remember Walter Payton*. A former newspaper reporter, he has written for the *Fort Worth Star-Telegram* and *The National*. Towle is president and publisher of TowleHouse Publishing Company, based in Nashville, Tennessee, where he lives with his wife, Holley, and their son, Andrew.

Printed in the USA
CPSIA information can be obtained
at www.ICGtesting.com
JSHW082207140824
68134JS00014B/483